To Tom

From Mom & Dad

Chapter XIV

History of Thein family

COME ALONG TO
LUXEMBOURG

COME ALONG TO
LUXEMBOURG

By

L. E. LEIPOLD, Ph.D.

Publishers

T. S. DENISON & COMPANY, INC.

Minneapolis

T. S. DENISON & COMPANY, INC.

Standard Book Number: 513-01250-8

Library of Congress Card Number: 72-77992

Printed in the United States of America
by The Brings Press

A LOOK AT LUXEMBOURG

When looking at this map, keep in mind that Luxembourg is a very small country. From north to south, it is only about sixty-two miles long. At its widest part, it is about thirty-seven miles in width. The mining district shown on the lower left part of the map is ten or twelve miles wide. The hot springs district at the bottom, right side of the map, is only two or three miles across. The wine-producing region shown in the southeastern section extends not more than about thirty or thirty-five miles along the Moselle River.

The old saying that good things often come in small packages certainly applies to Luxembourg!

Grand Duke Jean and Grand Duchess Josephine Charlotte

DEDICATION

To
His Royal Highness
GRAND DUKE JEAN
and to
Her Royal Highness
GRAND DUCHESS JOSEPHINE CHARLOTTE
Beloved by their people
this book is dedicated

CONTENTS

FOREWORD

The country to which you are invited to visit with me is a never-never land of castles and fortresses.

It is a Camelot and a Gibraltar, a happy land with a tragic past; a land of haunting beauty, of rugged crags and wooded hills. It is a country that has come into the twentieth century straight out of a medieval past.

A thousand years ago, Sigefroid, Count of Ardennes, built his castle on a great rock overlooking the Alzette River. It was called "Lucilinburhuc," from which the modern name of Luxembourg developed. Lucilinburhuc meant "Little Castle," the castle of Sigefroid. From that beginning the modern city and state of Luxembourg grew.

The old days of knights in armor and bold marauders bent on adventure are gone. Today one third of this land that is 999 square miles big is devoted to agriculture. Grapes grown along the Moselle River produce wine that is known throughout Europe and America for its excellence. Great steel mills have

The castle at Vianden. Luxembourg is dotted with many beautiful castles, of which this one is typical.

Castle of Wiltz—stage for an annual concert in July.

sprung up, the twelfth largest in the world. There is no unemployment to be found. During a recent year only seven persons were reported to be out of work.

The army, once a force of thousands to be reckoned with, now numbers only six hundred men. Centuries ago seven thousand soldiers manned the great fortress of Luxembourg City alone. Everyone can read and write in this busy little country. There is little or no prejudice or bigotry to be found here. Though almost all of the people are Roman Catholics, they recognize the right of others to their own beliefs. A good example of their sincerity was shown recently when the people helped a rabbi new to Luxembourg City to set up his synagogue.

In this small land of beauty and enchantment, it is easy to believe in bold deeds performed by armored knights of old; in kings and queens, and in brave princes and beautiful princesses. They were all here once upon a time; they live today in story and legend. For all that we know, the spirits still haunt the castles that dot the high hills of this country.

So come along with me to the fairyland called Luxembourg! It will be a happy visit, long remembered.

Chapter I

AN OLD, OLD COUNTRY

It is said that a tourist and his wife were driving through France.

"They told me in the last town that we went through that we were leaving France and coming to another country. What is its name?" asked the husband.

"I will look it up on the map," replied his wife.

"Never mind," said the husband. "We just went through it."

While this story is just a joke about Luxembourg's small size, it could be almost true. From the town of Mondorf les Bains in France across Luxembourg to the town of Remich, on the German border, it is only a couple of miles by road.

On a map of Europe, Luxembourg is hardly more than a dot. It lies wedged in by the three countries of France, Germany, and Belgium. To the south is France, to the east lies Germany, on the west and north is Belgium. The capital city bears the same

"The Three Towers." These towers are hundreds of years old.

The Castle of Colmar-Berg, the summer residence of the Grand Duke.

name as the country itself and it is in the southern section of the land, a few miles from the French border.

Since Luxembourg's reigning ruler is a grand duke, the country is called a grand duchy. Belgium, next-door neighbor, is a kingdom with a king at the head of its government. France and West Germany are both republics and their heads of state are presidents.

Luxembourg is small, but it is an old, old country. Almost two thousand years ago, when the great Roman general Julius Caesar led his army from Rome to the Rhine River, Germany's boundary, he was met by fierce resistance from the people of Luxem-

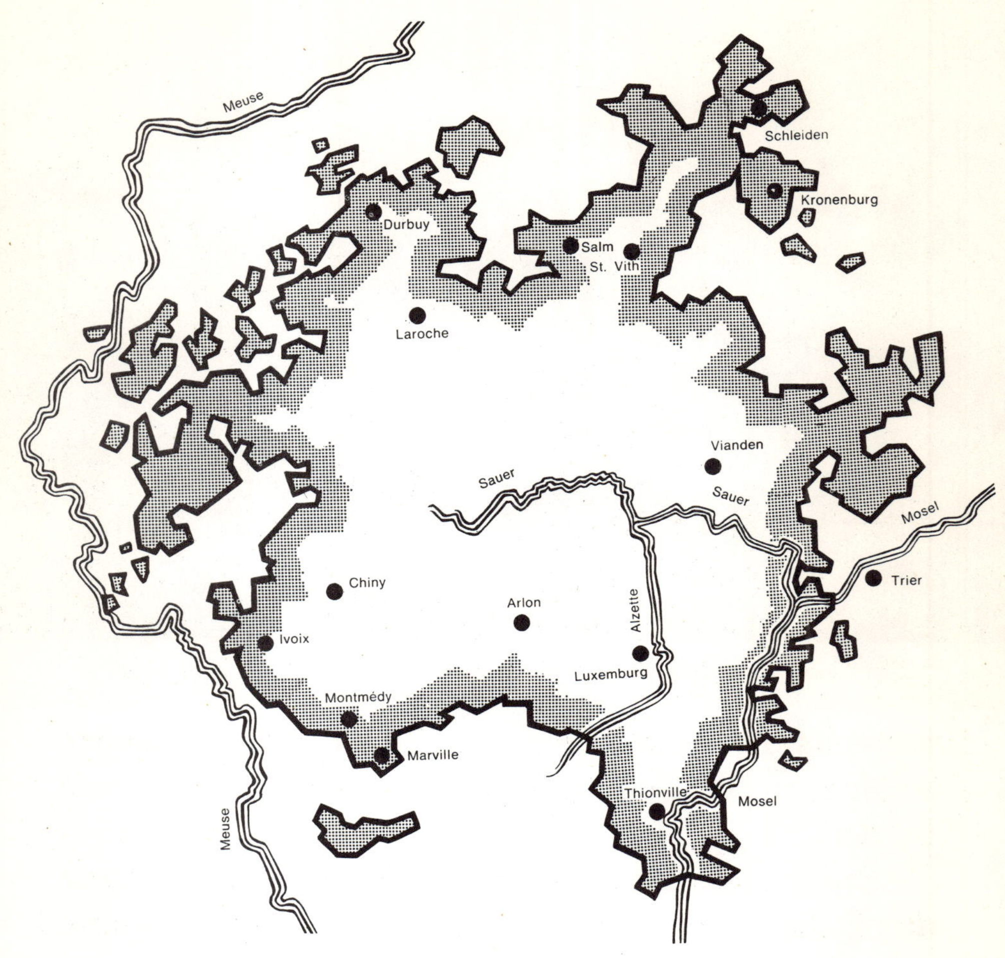

THE OLD DUCHY OF LUXEMBOURG
Luxembourg was never very large, even during its best years. This map shows how the old duchy once extended from the Moselle River on the east to the Meuse on the west. At that time it was almost three times its present size.

bourg. Caesar defeated them but never completely subdued them. They are just as determined today to be free and independent and to resist any attempt to control them as they were two thousand years ago.

View of Ettelbruck. The valleys of this little fairyland country are filled with beautiful towns such as this one.

Almost a thousand years after the Romans made the region a part of their great empire, Luxembourg became an independent nation with its own name and ruler. It was Sigefroid of the Ardennes family who founded Luxembourg. The Romans had built a fort where the capital city now stands, but by Sigefroid's time it had already fallen into ruins. In the year 963, he rebuilt this fort and around it grew a village that year by year grew in size and power, becoming known as Luxembourg.

Sigefroid was the ancestor of many famous men and women. One of them, Charles IV, became em-

The city of Echternach, an old, old city that dates back to Roman days.

peror of the great Holy Roman Empire; another, Henry VII, was emperor of Germany; William the Silent founded the Dutch Republic; John the Blind, a famous knight, was king of Bohemia; Ermesinde, countess of Luxembourg, was a saintly religious leader.

A tale is told to the Luxembourg children about Sigefroid and the founding of their country.

One day the knight Sigefroid was hunting in the Ardennes highlands which lie in the northern part of the little nation. As he made his way along the Alzette River as it wound its uneven way through the rugged valley, he came upon the ruins of an old castle built by the Romans on a great rock.

Suddenly he heard the sweet voice of a maiden singing an alluring song high up among the ruins. Looking up, he saw a beautiful girl. It was Melusine, fairy of the Alzette. Just then she saw Sigefroid and at once disappeared from view. So appealing was her voice that the knight could not forget it, returning time and again to the castle ruins to catch a glimpse of her and to listen to the beautiful strains of her voice which had so completely captivated him. He fell in love with her and begged her to marry him.

Melusine loved Sigefroid, too, and agreed to marry him, but she said that first he must promise her three things: she was never to leave the rock on which stood the ruined castle; he must promise that he would never try to see her on a Saturday; and

Castles at Clervaux. Some castles are in ruins, but these two are still in use.

finally, she was not to be questioned about what she did on Saturdays after they were married. Sigefroid readily agreed to the three conditions and they were married.

Sigefroid was sad because he was a penniless knight and had no money to build a splendid castle for his beautiful bride. In desperation, he made a pact with the Evil One, selling his soul to him in return for which he was to be given a fine castle. Satan indeed built him such a castle, for overnight it was erected on the big rock called the Bock, overlooking the Alzette River.

Hollenfels, youth hostel, one of many hostels that serve the young people of Luxembourg and visitors to the country.

The lovers were happy for a long time in their beautiful castle. However, Sigefroid's friends were envious of him and his lovely bride. They noticed that she was always absent on Saturdays and when they asked Sigefroid about it, he could not tell them where she went on those days. They hinted of strange reasons for her absence and planted doubts and suspicions in his mind. Sigefroid at first refused to listen to these wild tales, but his doubts grew until he determined to find out the truth for himself.

One Saturday shortly afterward, Sigefroid went stealthily to the door of his wife's apartment in the castle and listened, his ear to the door. From within came the sound of splashing water! Peering through the keyhole, he saw his beautiful bride bathing in rippling water, but to his horror she was now a mermaid with a fish's tail instead of legs! He cried out in dismay, upon which Melusine vanished. He had lost her forever!

Because Sigefroid had broken his word, his fairy bride became imprisoned in the rock upon which the castle stood. Every seven years since that tragic day she has come back, sometimes as the beautiful maiden that Sigefroid first beheld on the rock, sometimes in the form of a serpent. In the serpent's mouth is carried a golden key by which a brave knight could free her from her imprisonment.

This tale has been told to the children of Luxembourg for a thousand years. Someday, they are told,

Village of Esch-sur-Sure. Many people regard this little village as the most beautiful one in Luxembourg.

the beautiful Melusine will be saved from her unhappy fate.

Years passed. The stronghold of Sigefroid and Melusine gave its name to the town and the little kingdom that grew up around it. In time the village became a city and another wall had to be built to enclose all of the houses. The country that surrounded Luxembourg town also expanded its borders, taking in a region that was part of France. French became the language of the people of Luxembourg, mixing with the German spoken in the eastern section. Today the people speak a language

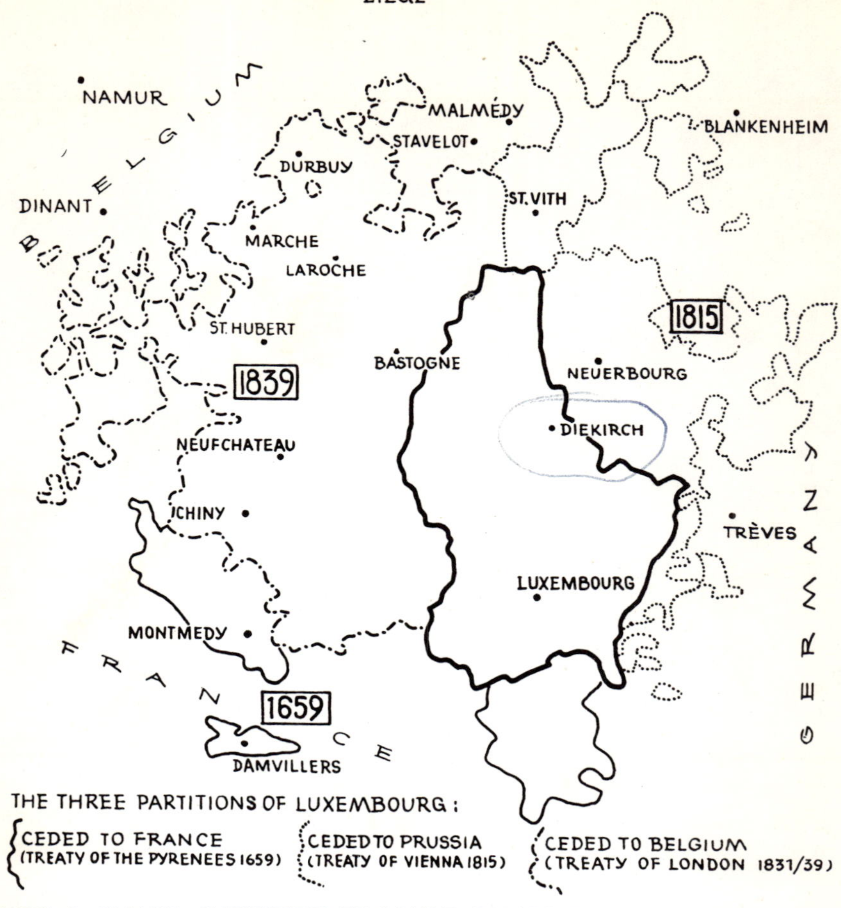

HOW A SMALL COUNTRY IS MADE SMALLER
The dismemberment of Luxembourg began in 1659 when France took from it the land around Thionville and Montmedy as shown on the above map. A century and a half later, Prussia took a generous slice of territory adjoining it. Luxembourg was powerless to resist its big neighbor and was forced to submit to the dismemberment. In 1839, Belgium seized more than half of the remaining land, leaving Luxembourg with its present boundaries. Today the Great Powers guarantee the duchy its independence.

that is a strange mixture of that of its two big neighbors.

Countess Ermesinde, who reigned for over fifty years, was a capable ruler. The size of Luxembourg increased three times over during her reign (1196 to 1247). She had the welfare of her people at heart

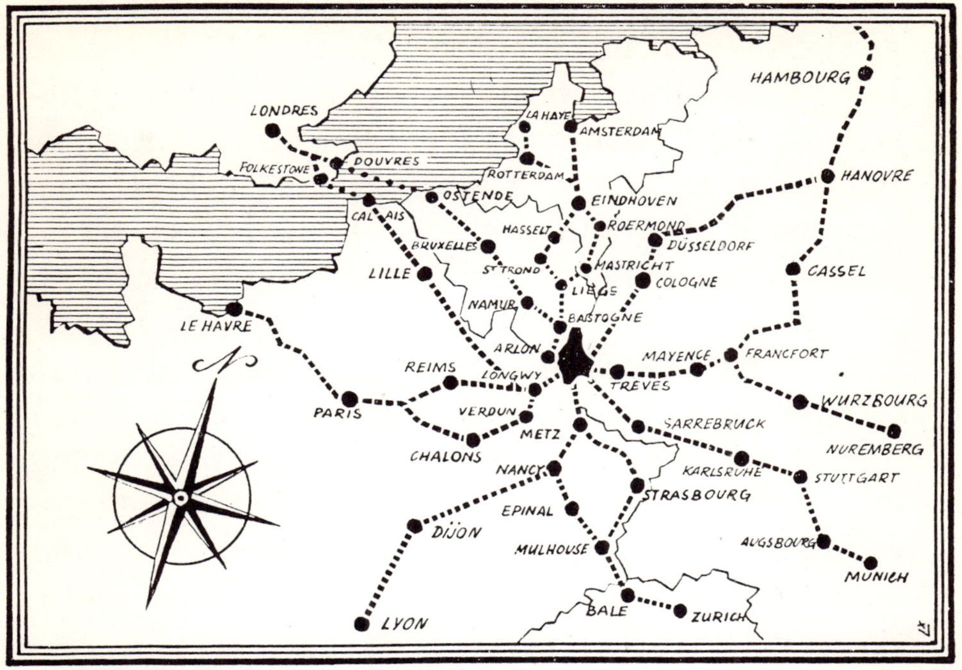

ALL ROADS LEAD TO LUXEMBOURG!
For two thousand years, the armies of Europe crossed and recrossed Luxembourg. Those were unhappy times for the people of the country. The above map shows its central location, roads leading out from it in all directions. Today armies are no longer marching, but almost as many tourists are footloose in the region. The people of Luxembourg welcome tourists to their land, for there is so much for them to see.

and provided many reforms for their benefit. She was one of the most enlightened rulers of her time, granting charters of freedom to such cities as Echternach, Luxembourg and Thionville.

The wise countess was succeeded by her son, Henry V, who possessed many of his mother's wise traits. His position was strengthened when the rich and powerful Count Vianden recognized him as the lawful ruler of Luxembourg.

Little Luxembourg now entered upon the most glorious period in its history. Henry VII succeeded Henry VI and he became emperor of the Holy Roman Empire, greatest of all the nations of Europe. Beneath him in power were the feudal lords who dominated the countryside about them. They sat in judgment over the villagers and serfs, their fortified strongholds defying others about them. Today many of these castles still remain as silent ruins, reminders of more glorious days that once were.

The Church was a powerful institution during these hectic years and the counts of Luxembourg were active in its behalf. They built monasteries and nunneries and supported them, some in the towns, others in the rural regions.

Like most noblemen of the time, they loved to fight and were frequently in conflict with their neighbors. In the year 1288, a bloody battle was fought at Worringen in which four brothers of the house of Luxembourg were slain, and this put an end to their warlike activities for some time.

Henry VII had been educated at the brilliant French court, this fact influencing his own court in the capital city of Luxembourg. For several generations this was the pattern followed, making the rulers of the little nation more influential than the size of their country warranted.

Only a year after Henry became Emperor of the Holy Roman Empire, he died, to be succeeded by his son John. At the time of his ascending to the throne,

Another castle, set amid the fields and forests of Septfontaines.

he was only fourteen years old. He quickly became mixed up in all of the current affairs of the time and traveled widely. His eyesight was very poor and blindness threatened. While leading his troops across Lithuania, he consulted a physician who did his best, but only made matters worse. Angered, John ordered the unfortunate doctor thrown into the Oder River and drowned.

Soon he was sightless, known as John the Blind. At the battle of Crecy in 1356, he entered the thick of the fray to help his ally, the King of France, against the English forces. The battle went against

Another scenic view, Esch-sur-Sure, in an incomparable setting.

them and he and almost all of his men were killed. His bravery was widely acclaimed. To honor the knightly John, the English Prince of Wales made the three ostrich feathers worn on John the Blind's helmet and his motto, "Ich dien" (I serve), a part of the insignia on his own coat of arms. To this day, it is to be found on the crest of the Prince of Wales. John the Blind, gallant and fearless knight, has, since his death, been Luxembourg's national hero.

The country expanded its borders during the rule of John's son, Charles IV (1346-1353), and that of Charles' brother, Wenceslas I (1353-1383). It was during the latter's reign that the country reached its greatest size.

Tragic times followed. Debts burdened the land, and to exact payment, conquest threatened. In 1443, Philip, Duke of Burgundy, invaded and conquered Luxembourg. For the next four hundred years it was part of first one country, then another. It belonged to Spain, then to Austria; twice it became a part of France.

The people of Luxembourg, however, never forgot that they were once independent. Stubbornly they clung to their customs and to their language. It was traditional for subjects of conquered nations to pledge allegiance to their conquerors by raising their right hand in a two-fingered salute. The Luxembourgers raised only *one* finger! Even the emperors of the mighty Holy Roman Empire, when giving the list of titles that they held, added ". . . and Duke of Luxembourg," thus recognizing the status of the little duchy.

Proud of their heritage and jealous of their independence, they survived four hundred years of conquest, to emerge once again as an independent nation in the nineteenth century.

Beaufort—the ruins of the castle.

Chapter II

UNDER FOREIGN RULE

When Philip the Good, Duke of Burgundy, conquered Luxembourg in 1443, the duchy lost its independence and became a province. For the next sixty-three years it was a part of Burgundy, passing in 1506 to Spain under whose rule it remained for over two centuries.

Because of its strategic position between France and the Rhine, the capital town of Luxembourg gradually changed from a medieval market town to a great stronghold to be reckoned with. In time it was to be known as the "Gibraltar of the North," strongest fortress in all western Europe. Strong fortifications guarded the approach to the city itself, within which were bulwarks and redoubts. Hewn out of the great rock on which the principal fortification rested were many miles of underground passageways, similar to those of the mighty Gibraltar itself which guarded the entrance to the Mediterranean Sea.

LIKE FATHER, LIKE SON
Philip the Good (left) and his son, Charles the Bold, two fifteenth-century rulers of Luxembourg. There was a remarkable resemblance between the two, as can be seen from these drawings.

The name of Luxembourg became associated with those of the greatest military commanders of Europe. Recognized as being the mighty fortress that it was, it took strong protective measures to live up to its name. Located far from the center of the city were the outworks, the protective walls and redoubts with their forts and bastions perched high on rocks so steep that they could not be scaled. The underground passageways led in all directions, here and there enlarged to become storerooms of supplies and ammunition.

The bridge Adolphe in the city of Luxembourg, often called "the city of bridges."

It was the military men of France, Spain and Austria who planned the defenses of the town. They would make it so strong that no enemy from the north or east—notably England or Germany—would ever dare to attack it. Wars raged about it for more than a hundred years, but it grew stronger with the passing of time. Often the inhabitants of the city were fewer in number than the soldiers who guarded them. Generals who were given the task of capturing the stronghold faced an almost hopeless task. After months of preparation and planning, more months went by besieging the outer walls. If they fell to the attackers, more and stronger defenses were met before the city itself was reached. Thick walls and sheer cliffs bristling with guns had to be reckoned with. Only through a long siege and eventual starvation of the garrison could success be hoped for.

After Spain wrested the little country from Burgundy in 1506, almost two centuries went by before it again changed conquerors. Then Louis XIV, the Grand Monarch of France, attacked the fortified city and, after suffering heavy losses through many battles, succeeded in capturing it. Louis did not desire it so much for himself as he dreaded others having so great a fortification. It was soon wrested from him by Spain, not to become a vassal of France again until Napoleon took it a century later.

Palace changing of the guards at the Grand-Ducal Palace.

To add to the misery that the military chiefs brought upon the people were the religious tribulations of the time. The Luxembourgers remained faithful to the Church of Rome, rejecting the Protestantism that swept through Germany and other countries of northern Europe. The people were ignorant and superstitious, preyed upon by the military and afflicted by repeated plagues which swept the country. Drastic ordinances by Spanish rulers discouraged either political revolution or religious reformation.

When the "Low Countries" to the north rebelled against their Spanish oppressors, the people of Luxembourg remained impassive. However, witchcraft hysteria swept the country which paid a frightful toll for its superstitions. Education remained at a low level throughout this period.

In spite of the hectic times, Luxembourg City grew in size and importance and imposing buildings graced its streets.

The period during the Thirty Years' War in the seventeenth century was a time of unusual tribulations for the people of Luxembourg. For some years before the beginning of the war, troops of several nations as well as "freebooters" devastated the country. With the entry of France into the war in 1635, conditions worsened. Troops repeatedly crossed and recrossed the land, burning villages and destroying

The town of Clervaux.

crops. To make matters worse, the war was followed by famine and epidemic.

For more than twenty-five years these desperate conditions afflicted the country. When a semblance of peace and order was restored, more than half the people were dead, victims of war and pestilence. Peace came eventually, but it proved to be only a prelude to other wars to come. Luxembourg was paying cruel penalty for being located amid the warring nations.

In spite of these bitter years of strife, the people remained staunch in their faith, and in 1666 they chose Our Lady, the Blessed Virgin, to be their coun-

A typical village square scene.

try's patroness. From that year on, a religious observance in the month of May has brought every parish in the country to the Luxembourg cathedral to thank Our Lady for her help and to implore her protection.

Because the city and the surrounding territory suffered so greatly during the four centuries that it remained under foreign control, there remains today only a small number of historic monuments of any beauty or value. Of even greater importance, the country continued to shrink in size as first one nation and then another took a slice of its territory. France began the partition in 1659 when it took from Luxembourg several pieces of land in the south. In 1815, Prussia took a big slice adjoining it to the east. More than half of what was left was annexed by Belgium twenty-four years later, leaving only a thousand square miles of territory to Luxembourg.

Today the country's boundaries remain as they were established at that time. However, the language of the Luxembourgers is still spoken in the areas that were taken from her by force. The will to remain a people is as strong as ever in these hardy folk.

The great Luxembourgian fortress that made the small country famous, begun by Sigefroid before the year 1000, grew with each conqueror until it covered more than four hundred and fifty acres. Within its strong walls were no fewer than twenty-four massive stone forts. In time the people of Luxembourg realized that their remarkable fortress had no value to

Enjoying fishing on a river.

Fishing in a mountain stream.

THE MIGHTY FORTRESS OF LUXEMBOURG
The fortress of Luxembourg grew stronger and stronger until there was none in Europe except Gibraltar that was more powerful. This drawing shows the formidable fortification in the eighteenth century, at its height. No nation really wanted it for its own as much as it wanted to keep other nations from possessing it.

them at all. Rather, it was a heavy burden. None of the great powers really wanted to possess the country, for it was a tiny one of farms and poor people. It was the powerful fortress that they wanted—and the only reason that each one desired it was to prevent one of the other countries from having it.

About a hundred years ago (1867), at a meeting of men from the great powers of Europe held in London, a way was found to solve the problem. The castle must be destroyed. No garrison would ever point its cannon at another army again. Eight countries agreed to the plan: Great Britain, France, the Netherlands, Prussia (the forerunner of modern Germany), Austria, Russia, Belgium, and Italy. At the same time that they agreed to demolish the fortress, they agreed to preserve Luxembourg's independence.

Prussia, which then occupied the place, withdrew its force of seven thousand men and the destruction began. For almost a thousand years it had stood on the rock overlooking the Alzette River. It had begun as a small fortress, built by Sigefroid. It had been the center of many great wars, contended for by armies from all directions. Now only ruins survived. It was the end of an era that would be no more. Today it is visited not by armies, but by tourists, curious to see the place that had played so important a part in the history of Europe.

With the withdrawal of the German troops, Luxembourg once more became a peaceful little country, content with its role. No longer did it aspire to greatness, for that era was passed. Now it had time to dream of the days that once were but would be no more.

Chapter III

LUXEMBOURG BECOMES A MODERN STATE

The history of the modern Grand Duchy of Luxembourg began in 1815 when a congress of representatives of the great powers of Europe met in Vienna, Austria. The continent had for many years been torn apart by the armies of Napoleon, intent upon becoming the master of Europe. At Waterloo, in Belgium, he had met disaster and his ambitions crumbled about him, just as his empire did. The Congress of Vienna met to restore some semblance of order to the continent.

Luxembourg lost much of its land through decisions made by others. The map on page 26 shows the area taken from her in 1815. The people, their language and customs, remained the same, but they were now subjects of Germany. A greater blow was to fall later, in 1839, when more than half of what remained of Luxembourg was taken by Belgium.

Residence at Echternach.

Camping scene in Luxembourg.

The thousand square miles that remained were but a remnant of the once powerful state. So it has remained to this day.

Some people believe that Luxembourg has no real reason for existing at all, that it should belong to a larger nation. It exists today, they say, simply because none of the great powers would permit any other country to take it. This belief the people of Luxembourg firmly deny. They are a nation because they deserve to be one, they claim. They are a people in their own right, being neither French, German nor Belgian. They have their own language, their own customs and their own national heritage.

Folk dancing on the town square.

The venerable Joseph Bech, when he was Foreign Minister of Luxembourg, said when World War II was in progress and his country was occupied by German troops, that it has often been said—and especially by German writers wishing to serve their own selfish purposes—that the Grand Duchy is only a creation of other nations. This is not true, he stated. From the fifteenth century onwards, Luxembourg has been a distinct nation, even when under the control of other nations, such as Burgundy, Spain and Austria, he pointed out.

Supporting Mr. Bech was an English authority who wrote, "Surrounded by France, Germany and

Belgium, this little country is neither French, German nor Belgian. It has a distinct physical, social and ethnical character of its own."

When the Great Powers of Europe agreed that Luxembourg should be a free and independent nation in spite of its small size, they merely recognized an historical fact. That it exists as a free and independent country is truly remarkable. The people have developed and kept their own language and it is spoken not only in what is Luxembourg today, but in an area four times that large. The will to live free is strong in the people of Luxembourg, just as it has been for hundreds of years.

During much of the nineteenth century—from 1810 to 1890—the kings of Holland were also the grand dukes of Luxembourg. In 1890, the Grand Duchy began its own dynasty, that of the House of Nassau-Weilbourg. Grand Duke Adolphe was the first of that line, reigning until 1910. The present grand duke is Jean, son of the grand duchess, Charlotte, who ruled the land for forty-five years. He married Princess Josephine-Charlotte of Belgium, sister of the king of that country.

In 1914, war broke out in Europe, and Luxembourg suffered ill effects when the armies of the German Kaiser occupied not only it but Belgium and Holland as well. The people of the occupied territory bided their time and in 1918 they were liberated by the French and Americans, our troops being under

A scene in the thousand-year-old Luxembourg City "La Citadelle du St. Esprit."

the command of General "Black Jack" Pershing. More than three thousand Luxembourg soldiers, most of them fighting under the flags of the United States and France, gave their lives for their country in this war.

Following the close of the war, the country entered upon a period of unusual prosperity. The standard of living became increasingly higher and good times prevailed. It was too good to last, a lull before the storm. In 1939, World War II broke out and all the savagery of modern warfare was loosed upon the hapless little nation. Located as it was between two of the Great Powers, it was one of the first victims of Adolf Hitler's mighty military machine. On

Sailing on Upper Sure Lake.

May 10, 1940, the invasion began. Luxembourg was once again being ground under the heel of an oppressor, as it had been so many times in the past.

The Grand Duchess Charlotte and her family fled to England and the members of the government sought refuge likewise in friendly countries, including America. Meanwhile, in Luxembourg a German governor appointed by Hitler ruled the country. Freedom of speech and the press were done away with and many people were imprisoned. An attempt by Hitler to induce all Luxembourgers to sign a statement declaring that they were actually Germans ended in failure. This they resolutely refused to do. Other demands were made until conditions became intolerable. A general strike was called and resistance against the invaders spread throughout the country. Little Luxembourg did what no other nation had as yet dared to do—defy the great German "Wehrmacht." Many people were shot, many more deported to other lands. Yet the proud Luxembourgers continued to resist the invaders.

After almost five years, liberation came. When the people saw Grand Duke Jean among the first American soldiers to enter the capital city, they went wild with joy. Their country was once more freed from the heel of an oppressor. A new and better day had dawned for their little nation, the people sensed. They had survived conquest and emerged victorious. Thousands of their men had died during the war years and countless other Luxembourgers had been deported to other lands. It would take many years to recover from the war's ill effects.

On November 12, 1964, Grand Duchess Charlotte gave up the throne in favor of her son, Prince Jean. She had reigned for forty-five years. He reigns today as Grand Duke Jean of Luxembourg.

Grand-Ducal Palace in the city of Luxembourg.

Chapter IV

THIS LAND CALLED LUXEMBOURG

There are 335,000 people living in the Grand Duchy of Luxembourg, sixty-two miles from north to south and thirty-seven miles from east to west, at its widest points. In this small land there is a surprising amount of variety in the scenery.

The southern part of Luxembourg is a plains region, quite level, but in places, with low, rolling hills. The northern and western sections are hilly, almost mountainous, with many streams and deep valleys. The tops of these high hills are rugged and wooded; the slopes are steep and the glens between them are narrow and winding.

The plains region is filled with small farms, most of them of thirty or forty acres. In America a farm is considered small if it is only eighty acres in size; in Luxembourg there are few farms that large.

Folklore March. During its long history, many traditions have developed, some of which are carried on today.

The hilly part of the country is known to the natives as the "E'sleck" and farming is difficult there. The land from ancient times was not fertile. When steel mills were built in southern Luxembourg in the nineteenth century, fertilizer became a by-product of the mills and the farmers of the E'sleck began to use it on their land. Today they are more prosperous because of it.

Many villages are found in the E'sleck, clinging to the hillsides or nestled snugly in the valleys. There are many people living in the valleys who seldom see the sun for more than a few hours a day, for it hides behind the steep walls and the cliffs except during the few hours at midday.

A beautiful country estate at Mondorf-les-Bains.

French is the official language of the government, but most people speak "Luxembourgish" or as it is more popularly called, "Letzeburgesch." It is a language of its own, used more as a spoken language than as a written one. More and more people are becoming familiar with English, and a traveler from America can find someone who can understand him and reply to his questions in English in many of the villages.

Although Luxembourg is not located near the ocean, it is nevertheless affected by it. Winds that blow from the west give it a moderate climate, seldom extreme. The summers are pleasant; the winters mild. The air is often humid, however, resulting in plenty of rainfall, especially in the southern portion. There are considerable weather changes, some seasonal, some even on a day-to-day basis, but seldom or never is the weather really rigorous.

Because of the rugged beauty of much of the country—the area around Echternach is known as "Little Switzerland"—many tourists are attracted to the area. Youth hostels are abundant, providing a night's lodging for only a few pennies. Some of the hostels are old castles, romantically linking the present to the heroic past. In addition, there are rest houses, holiday homes and campgrounds which provide visitors with good places to stay.

Visitors, old and young, are always welcome in Luxembourg, and are treated with respect and courtesy. The people of this pleasant little country are quiet and friendly, always ready to pass the time of day with a stranger. As travelers from other lands learn more about this country, they are attracted to it, many of them returning year after year. They enjoy the historic towns and castles and the wild, wooded valleys. Perhaps, above all, they enjoy the peaceful serenity that lies over the land. The days of armies marching over the Luxembourg hills are now gone, a part of the past. Peace reigns where once the roar of cannons broke the tranquil stillness.

Chapter V

THE REGIONS OF LUXEMBOURG

THE E'SLECK

The plains of southern Luxembourg gradually give way to the highlands of the north. They are not great towering mountains like our Rockies, but they have a beauty all their own. At best they are no higher than eighteen hundred feet, but they are true ranges, with rugged crests, twisting and squirming about, their steep slopes leading into shady glens. Everywhere are evergreens of the spruce family, mixed here and there with sturdy oak trees.

The cut-up, rugged land of northern Luxembourg makes poor farming, with much of the land too rough and hilly for crops. However, newer methods of farming are helping to make the farmers more prosperous than they once were. Today about a third of the people of the land make their living by farming.

The E'sleck is a part of the Ardennes highland region, spilling over into Luxembourg from neighboring Belgium. The beauty of the region is such

In southern Luxembourg are some of the largest steel smelting plants in the world.

that it appeals to hikers and to those people who love the out-of-doors. Trails lead into the hills, taking hikers from the valleys to the hill crests which provide breathtaking views. Below the barren peaks lie picturesque valleys dotted with homes of farmers. Countless villages nestle among the hills, in appearance much as they have been for centuries.

Castles, built in bygone days, many of which are a thousand years old, now lie in ruins, gracing the hilltops. Roads that lead in and out of the valleys are everywhere. Here one goes up a steep incline, over there another descends sharply into a valley and disappears among the trees. They follow the winding Sure and Our rivers, swinging around jutting rocks, passing neat, white farmhouses, losing themselves among the hills. Who built the roads and when, nobody knows. They have been here longer than the oldest inhabitant can remember; they were here when his parents and grandparents lived in the snug house that is now his. Time goes on and on and the hills of Luxembourg change but little.

Most of the castles are in ruins, but even so, their scattered stones tell of a wild, romantic past. They belonged to families, many of whose names were known throughout Europe. They were counts and dukes and barons whose actions did not always befit their noble claims. They had little respect for the common people, the serfs, and often they made the lives of these lesser people miserable.

Travelers were at the mercy of each castle lord through whose land they passed. The landed barons were generally a rough lot, spoiling for a fight. They liked excitement and went out of their way to look for it. Strangers were always regarded as ready victims, to be taken advantage of. Often they would be robbed of their possessions and turned loose, penniless.

Each baron was jealous of other noblemen, with the result that they warred upon each other almost constantly. The monasteries, too, were preyed upon, never safe from attack. Small wonder that today most of the once-strong castles lie in ruins, grim reminders of the warlike nature of their owners and of the hectic days of knighthood.

On the eastern border between Luxembourg and Germany, is the town of Vianden. Many years ago the counts of Vianden were among the strongest noble families of Luxembourg. Their castle was one of the finest in the region. Its huge hall of the knights could hold five hundred men. It is still fairly well preserved, an excellent example of what the finest of medieval castles was like.

It was at Vianden that many famous people of that day gathered, to be entertained royally. Scholars and musicians were always welcome, for although many of the nobles of that time were ignorant and crude, the counts of Vianden were a step above the average.

The last representative of the House of Vianden, the noblewoman Adelaide, married Othon of Nassau-Dillenburg in the fourteenth century. From this dynasty, later intermarried with the House of Orange, the present Grand Duke Jean and his family are descended.

There were other barons of the region, those of Esch on the Sure, of Brandenbourg and of Bourscheid, whose castles were smaller, but because they were located on high hills, were true strongholds. These nobles were powerful and respected.

The ruins of these once-great castles that time alone could conquer, give travelers in Luxembourg a good idea of what such strongholds were once like. The ramparts, now moss-covered, and the stone towers, green with ivy, cause visitors to marvel at what life was like when knights ruled the land. The rubble that was once rampart and battlement is now only a symbol of the past, a grim reminder of the tragedy of vanity and greed, for in time it all has become as nothing.

There was solitude in the E'sleck that lured not only noblemen, but also churchmen and their close kin, the monks, to it. Deep in the E'sleck wilderness they built monasteries that prospered and grew famous as the years went by, such as that of St. Hubert and Orval. They were founded in the early Middle Ages and quickly became centers of religious life and culture. They taught the people not only how to

Harvesting grain. Luxembourg is still essentially an agricultural nation.

prepare for the life to come, but also how to do better farming and how to read and write.

The powerful Knights Templar, an order which was widespread even beyond the boundaries of Europe, built a castle as strong as a fortress near Vianden and there they spread the cause of Christiandom, using their swords as well as the Bible. Travelers often used these monasteries and other religious centers as stopping places when journeying away from home.

Many such places were built hundreds of years ago, but on a lonely peak near Clervaux, the Order of St. Benedict built a splendid structure in 1909. In appearance it is much like the monasteries built seven or eight hundred years earlier. Travelers are always welcome here; at least they were until Hitler's forces came and drove the monks out. The monastery then became an Adolf Hitler School, the church building being converted into a gymnasium. Fortunately, when Hitler lost the war, the monks came back to their monastery.

Once upon a time it was unsafe to travel about in Europe and travelers were few and far between. After World War I (1918) more and more people took to the Luxembourg roads, usually on foot, enjoying the beautiful scenery of the E'sleck. Hotels became common even in the small towns and villages, their good food attracting many people. Especially was this true of such towns as Diekirch, Vianden and Wiltz. There were always such delicious items as venison, trout and smoked ham on the hotel menus. Along the Moselle fine wines and brandies were served.

Even the government helped to spread the fame of Luxembourg. A campaign was put on that extended across the ocean to America, telling the people of other countries of the many attractions of their little country. Especially was the region called the E'sleck popular, each of its many small towns and villages having its own special appeal to visitors.

THE GOOD LAND

When visiting Luxembourg, one is quick to note that it is divided quite well into two sections. About

Modern farming equipment is in use on many farms.

one half of the country is rough highlands, called the E'sleck. The southern half is more level, of low rolling hills and wide valleys. This part of Luxembourg is called "the Good Earth or "the Good Land."

When a traveler leaves the rough E'sleck and comes upon the Good Land, it is a real surprise. One moment he is in a wild region cut up by many glens and valleys; the next, he sees spread before him green fields and pastures, broken here and there by heavy woods.

Each of the valleys was formed in some distant past by the river that flows through it. There is the valley of the Alzette and the Attert, of the Mamer and the Eisch and the Moselle. They all have one thing in common, an idyllic peacefulness. That is the only resemblance, one to another. In other ways, each one is different from all the others.

Take the valley of the Alzette, for example. It is one of the widest of them all, almost a plain with the meandering Alzette flowing through its fields and meadows. Along its banks are willows and poplars, just as they are found along our own streams. The land away from the river is divided into many patches, reminding us that Luxembourg is a land of many small farms.

Though most of the farms are only thirty or forty acres in size, they are, nonetheless, more prosperous looking than those that were seen in the E'sleck. The houses and barns are larger and roomier, the soil is richer and the crops better than up north.

The Alzette flows northward, other rivers joining it along the way, its waters eventually reaching the Moselle and the busy Rhine.

The only two true cities of Luxembourg, Esch-on-Alzette and the capital, are on the Alzette. Esch is an industrial town of great steel mills and iron mines, providing prosperity for many Luxembourgers. It passes other towns, too, from small villages to larger centers. Bettembourg is a dairy town; Mersch has a well-preserved castle that now serves as a youth hostel; at Colmar-Berg is located the summer home of Grand Duke Jean and his family; Ettelbruck has a very good agricultural school.

The woods that cover the rolling hills are well kept and clean, for the people love to roam through them on winding paths. Now and then a deer is seen, surprised by the approach of a human being. There are other animals, too, which are seen in the woods, among them wild boar, just as there were when the Romans first crossed these hills and valleys two thousand years ago—and perhaps even for countless years before that.

The forest is never-ending, though broken often by fields and meadows. Fully one third of the nine hundred and ninety-nine square miles of Luxembourg is covered by trees. Records show that a century and a half ago, three fourths of the country were forest land. As the population grew in number, it became necessary to place more and more land under cultivation, until today there is more than twice as much land producing crops than there was then.

The valleys of the Attert, the Eisch and the Sure are similar to the Alzette in that they are all picturesque. Green fields, often outlined by thick forests, are everywhere. Here and there are the ruins of old castles and mansions, telling tales of days when bold knights roamed the land. In the Eisch Valley are the Seven Castles—Hollenfels, Schoenfels, Mersch, Koerich, Septfontaines, and the two Ansembourgs, old and new. The people who live near these old castles tell thrilling tales of hidden treasures, of goblins, and hair-raising ghost stories that tell all too

Wine making is a major industry in the Moselle Valley.

well why the valley is called the "Land of Haunted Castles."

THE MOSELLE VALLEY

Coming up from France and forming part of the eastern boundary of Luxembourg is the Moselle River. Leaving Luxembourg, it flows into Germany to join the Rhine at Coblenz. The beautiful valley of the Moselle is the wine-producing part of the country, the riverbanks lined with vineyards. Nearby hills and slopes are terraced and, when viewed from a distance, look like giant steps. The climate here is pleasant and the people who live in the valley are jovial.

Harvesting grapes as the quiet Moselle River flows by.

As far back as the time of the Romans, the Moselle Valley has been famous for its excellent wine. It is a "dry" wine; that is, not sweet, the kind preferred by so many people with their dinners.

The lives of the people of the valley were uneventful during times of peace, each year following the one before it with no special events of interest. The late spring of the year 1940 saw this changed, suddenly and tragically. The great war began and Luxembourg was one of its first victims. The sound of battle broke the peace of the valley and it would be five years before the burden of war was taken from them.

The vineyards that grew the winemakers' grapes had always taken much work to keep them in good condition. This the people had done without complaint. It was their lot to raise grapes and they accepted it. It was what the soil and climate of their valley produced best. The vineyards, however, needed almost constant care. They must be hoed and kept free of weeds; the vines must be trimmed and pruned. All this was expected, but the burden of war that was placed upon them was often too great to bear.

Many families were uprooted from their homes and forced to go elsewhere to work in some war factory that produced guns or ammunition. Others were deported to distant places at the will of the Nazi invaders. Thousands of them died in the struggle, for many men were forced to serve in the German army. It was a very unhappy time for those who lived in the Moselle Valley. They could only hope that the warlords of Germany would be defeated so that peace and quiet would be their lot once again.

It came when Hitler's forces were crushed between the Allied army of French, British and American soldiers on the western front and the Russian army on the eastern battle line. It was a long and costly war, but anything was better than to live in a world controlled by the Nazis. In April 1945, peace came and the guns were silenced in the valley.

Picking grapes, some of which are being enjoyed by the pickers!

The months that followed were uneasy ones, for it was no small task to restore order in a just manner after chaos had ruled for so long. Long after the fighting ended, a peace treaty was signed and Luxembourg was once again a free nation, her rights guaranteed by the big powers of Europe.

Another treaty was made and signed by France and Germany eleven years later. In October 1956, it was agreed upon by both countries. These two nations had long been traditional enemies and had fought three disastrous wars within a period of seventy years. They now were determined to be friends, ending the age-old enmity.

Boating on the Moselle River. Like the Rhine into which it flows, the Moselle is ever busy.

One of the provisions of the treaty provided that France and Germany should be connected by means of a canal, the Moselle River to become a part of it. It was to extend from Metz in France to Coblenz in Germany. This meant that the Moselle along the Luxembourg border had to be deepened and widened so as to be navigable for large riverboats.

The Luxembourg government was consulted to see if such a plan was satisfactory to it. It readily agreed and the work was begun. It was now the year 1961. Three years later the job was completed and the Moselle had a "new look." The river water was regulated by a system of dams. At several places electric power plants had been built, providing power for the inhabitants of the region. Port facilities were constructed at Mertert. Shipping is now easier for the winegrowers along the river canal. Slowly the life of the people is being made better because of the new waterway.

THE SOUTHERN REGION

Because Luxembourg is small and has many people, its land is very valuable. In the south of the country, along the French border, it is of especially high value, but not because it is such good farmland. This is the Land of the Red Earth, made red by the large amount of iron ore that it contains. All along the southern border, from Rodange on the southwestern border to Dudelange on the southeastern tip, a heavy layer of iron ore stretches across the land of Luxembourg. It has become a source of great wealth to the little nation.

About a century ago, the discovery was made that this iron ore had great value. Since ancient times the people of Luxembourg were quite poor, dependent upon the thin soil to provide a living for themselves. This it was not able to do, so many people left the country, immigrating to other lands, but principally to America. The cheap and abundant land of the Midwest made that region a real bonanza to the land-starved settlers.

The development of the steel industry changed all of that. Now there was work for everyone in the

Manufacturing heavy equipment.

Industry in Luxembourg.

Testing rail equipment.

Steel manufacturing is an important industry in Luxembourg.

More steel fabrication.

Modern industry in Luxembourg.

huge mills that sprang up along the French border. A by-product of the mills was a fertilizer which enriched the soil on the farms. All of the people benefited from the new industry. They now have one of the highest standards of living of any nation in the world. There is no unemployment in Luxembourg and people no longer desire to leave the country to go to some foreign land.

Of Luxembourg's 340,000 people, 25,000 are employed in the steel mills, thus making the steel industry the largest employer in the country. The principal plants are in Esch on the Alzette, a city of 30,000 people, next to the capital city in size.

Heavy industry tends to make a region prosperous, but it has its bad effects, too. All around Esch great clouds of smoke pour from the steel mills' stacks, fouling the air for miles around. Outside the mills are huge piles of waste earth and rock, "strippings" scraped from the surface to get at the good ore beneath. Miles of treeless, grassless open-pit mines provide a scene of desolation. These are some of the prices that must be paid for prosperity.

In the big office of the steel company is a modern computer that stands in an air-conditioned room, free from the dust that is found everywhere else about the plant. This machine is used for many purposes, from figuring the purity of the steel that is being produced from iron ore to determining the salaries of the company's employees.

Chapter VI

LITTLE JOURNEYS IN LUXEMBOURG

The best way to see the Duchy of Luxembourg is to hike or bicycle down its roads and trails. However, most people will not be able to spend that much time in the country, so automobile trips are next best. Eight of such trips are suggested to you. They are not long, the shortest being of less than seventy-five miles, and the longest, of a hundred and ten miles.

Kilometers are used instead of miles in Luxembourg. By multiplying the number of kilometers by .6, it can be readily changed to miles. To be more exact, multiply by .62. For example, 10 kilometers equals 6.2 miles; 100 kilometers is the same as 62 miles.

On each of the eight trips, something different will be seen. One takes the traveler through the E'sleck or highlands, another through the Moselle wine region, a third through the busy steel mill coun-

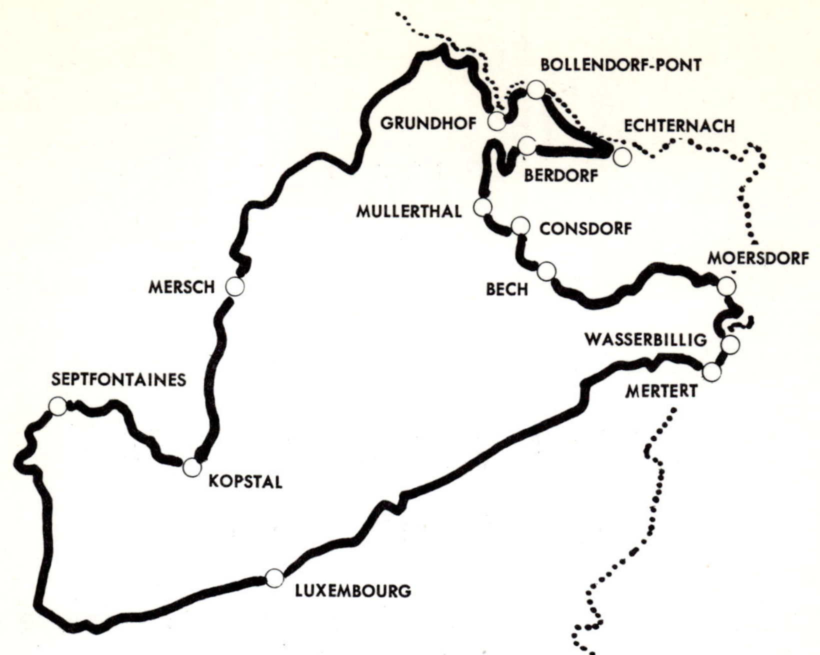

try in the southern section. Take all eight of these little journeys and one will see Luxembourg completely, its woods and mountains, its cities and villages, its winding streams and its castles.

One will go through many little villages that lie between those that are given on the maps. In fact, in Luxembourg one is seldom out of sight of one. Sometimes five or six can be seen at one time! Then again, some villages are so completely hidden in a dense woods or a deep glen that one comes upon them by complete surprise.

Little Journey No. 1—170 kilometers (105 miles)

We start at the capital city of Luxembourg, described in Chapter VII, and travel eastward to the Moselle Valley, through small villages and farms. Soon the twenty miles to the valley have been covered and we are in Mertert, a village of eight hundred people, with an inviting park. Just beyond lies Germany, across the river. Vineyards line the banks. At nearby Wasserbillig, about twice the size of Mertert, the Sure River joins the Moselle on its way to the Rhine. Just a short distance beyond are two villages of several hundred inhabitants, Born and Moersdorf, that have all the charm of the Old World.

Orchards line the roadsides and the banks of the Sure, for this is the center of the fruit-growing region of Luxembourg. Beck is a charming village of four hundred people in the "Little Switzerland" of Luxembourg, surrounded by orchards. In the nearby woods, wild game can be hunted. Here we pass the famous Bildchen sanctuary and its big oak tree, over a thousand years old.

We next come to Consdorf with its thousand inhabitants, a picturesque holiday resort. At nearby Mullerthal—population 60—we find ourselves in the heart of the Moellerdall, also known as "Little Switzerland," with wooded glens and ravines and valleys all about us. The road winds on through Berdorf to Echternach, which is described in another chapter. Perhaps we can someday visit here on Whit Tuesday and see the fantastic "Sprang-prozession!"

Beaufort is located on a little plateau in the Moellerdall. A medieval castle, now a picturesque ruin, was built in the eleventh century. Also to be seen is a more modern manor, built six hundred years later. The road winds on through tiny villages to Mersh, in the very center of Luxembourg. It is a town of fifteen hundred people, at the junction of the valleys of three rivers, the Alzette, the Mamer, and the Eisch. Gently rolling hills are seen all about. A castle, built a thousand years ago, then destroyed and later rebuilt, is next visited. Going southward a few miles, Kopstal is reached, located in the center of a wooded area with many fine paths for hiking. Little Septfontaines in the wooded Eisch Valley is dominated by the ruins of a once-great castle.

We proceed to Luxembourg City, our starting point. We have covered a little more than a hundred miles and have seen so much that our minds are filled with the beauty of it all. It has been a wonderful day! Tomorrow will bring new thrills.

Little Journey No. 2—150 kilometers (93 miles)

Let us begin our journey today at Echternach, which we visited yesterday. We go through Bergdorf and Beaufort in the beautiful Moellerdall and continue on to historic Vianden. This village of fifteen hundred is perhaps the most famous beauty spot in Luxembourg. The history of Vianden goes back over a thousand years. The beautiful castle was one of the largest feudal castles of Europe and today it has no equal west of the Rhine River.

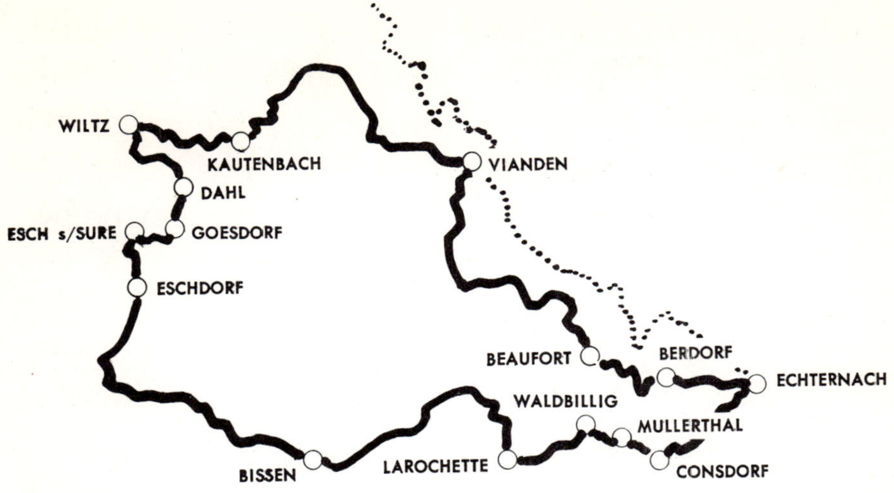

There is a folklore museum in Vianden which contains priceless items of furniture and other items of many years ago. The French poet Victor Hugo was exiled from France for some time, living his exiled years in Vianden. The house in which he lived is now the Victor Hugo Museum. In the restored old Trinitarian cloister is an interesting display of tombstones of the nobility of old Vianden. A "lift" takes visitors to a height of over thirteen hundred feet, providing splendid views of the surrounding area. The great castle is floodlighted every evening.

From Vianden we go to the little village of Kautenbach, situated in the hills of the Ardennes forest. In the surrounding woods are many paths for hikers, some of them leading to the nearby Schuttbourg castle. Kautenbach is an ideal place to rest and relax.

Now we come to one of the most spectacular villages of Luxembourg, little Esch-sur-Sure. It is a quiet little village of only three hundred or so inhabitants, a market town located on a spectacular site, almost completely surrounded by the Sure River. Its houses cluster around massive crags, the overall location dominated by the ruins of an old castle. It is a sheer drop to the Sure River, far below. As small as it is, it is never to be forgotten by any visitor, nor will it be by us.

At nearby Eschdorf, not much larger than Esch, we are up higher, providing a view over the countryside that is one of the wildest in the country. We continue on to Bissen in the Attert Valley. This is a peaceful region with many woods paths to follow among the beech and pine trees. East of us lies Larochette, a market town of a thousand people, as quaint as any that we have seen today. Two ancient castles of the eleventh and twelfth centuries dominate the romantic valley. We go on through Waldbillig in the Moellerdall to Consdorf, which we visited yesterday. From there it is but a short drive to Echternach, our starting point.

So ends our second tour. What a wonderful day it has been! Where else could we have seen so much, and on such a short trip of only ninety miles.

Little Journey No. 3—155 kilometers (97 miles)

Today we will start our journey at Clervaux, population 1000, and the principal town of northern Luxembourg. Clervaux is located in a deep, narrow

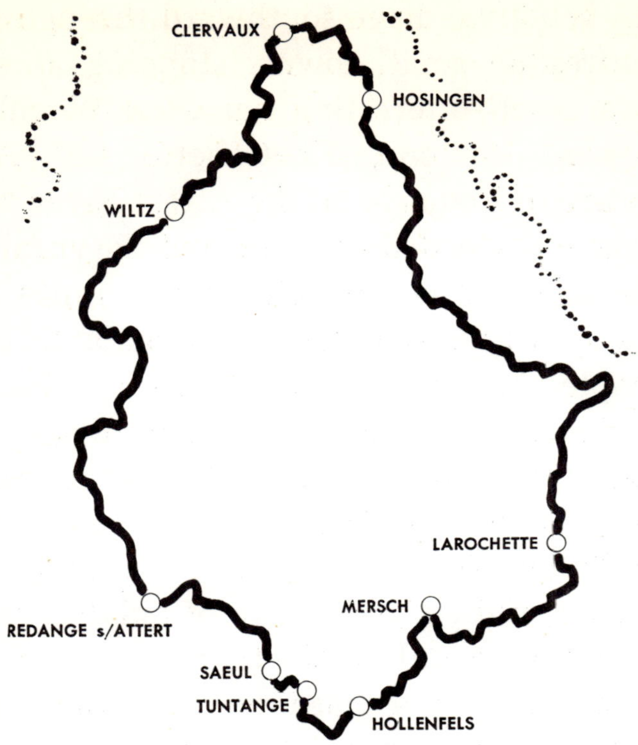

valley in the Ardennes region. A medieval castle is the first place that we visit, heavily damaged in World War II. If we could stay till evening, we are told that the castle, the abbey, the church and the chapel are all beautifully lighted up, but we make our apologies and drive on. Our drive takes us over winding roads to Wiltz, a larger town, several times the size of Clervaux. Although much of the town lies in a valley, there is also an upper town on the hill-tops above the valley. Here, as in Clervaux, is a fairy-land castle that looks out over the countryside from high up on the hills. From here we notice that the town has an airfield, much used by tourists.

From Wiltz we drive southward through numerous picturesque small towns, stopping at several. They bear such interesting names as Neunhausen, Lultzhausen, Bavigne, Koetschette and Arsdorf. Soon we are in Redange on the Attert River, a pleasant village in a wooded area. Most of the rural people here are farmers, we are told. A few miles farther on is Saeul, a typical village of perhaps three hundred people. All around the village, a dense forest thrives. Saeul is truly an Old World village.

We go on, passing villages every few miles. There is Tuntange, a village of three hundred and fifty people, and Hollenfels, with only half that number, and Ansembourg, with a population of only sixty. However, it has a feudal castle that was built in the twelfth century and a more modern manor built in 1639. One of the most romantic youth hostels in Luxembourg is the Hollenfels castle. What a thrill it would be to stay overnight in a real castle where knights and their ladies once lived!

On our first journey we visited Mersch, in the very center of Luxembourg, and we are glad to see it again. We are now in gently rolling hills, beautifully wooded. Again we drive through Larochette, a quaint old market town surrounded by woods. It has not one castle, but two, though both are in ruins.

We now go northward toward our morning's starting point, stopping at the village of Hosingen, a picturesque place—but aren't all of the villages of Luxembourg picturesque?

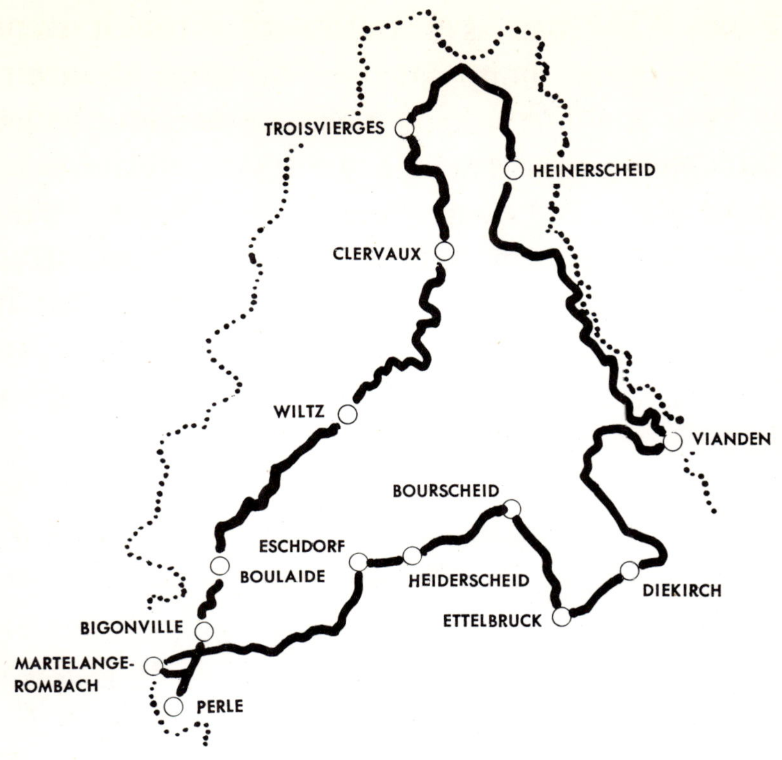

When we reach Clervaux, our starting point, we have covered almost a hundred miles. In America this distance would take less than two hours to cover, but it has taken us all day. There has been so much to see and besides, the roads are not exactly suited to fast driving! We have found, too, that the faster we drive, the less we see.

Little Journey No. 4—180 kilometers (111 miles)

As long as we ended yesterday's journey at Clervaux, let us start from there today. We will take a different road to Wiltz, passing through some rugged country. The road is a constant series of curves, seemingly never being straight for more than a few feet. This is typical Ardennes countryside. In spite of the slow speed at which we travel, Wiltz is soon in sight with its Lower Town in the valley and its Higher Town on the hill, with its big castle. Going on over winding roads, we soon come to Boulaide with its woods and lofty crags in the lonely forest of Ardennes. Just beyond it lies Bigonville, a quiet little village which is only a mile or so from the wild valley of the Sure River.

South of Bigonville we turn right on a side road to go to the village of Martelange-Rombach. It has one of the longest names in Luxembourg and very few inhabitants, only a hundred or so. It is located in the valley of the Sure, while nearby Perle is on a plateau. Both villages are surrounded by typical Ardennes landscape of rocks, ravines and lush pastures.

From here we turn eastward through woods and pastures to Eschdorf and Heiderscheid, both small villages on plateaus, offering wonderful views of the surrounding countryside.

At Bourscheid are the impressive ruins of the castle that was once one of the grandest for many miles around. It stands on a steep hill, almost five hundred feet above the wild valley of the Sure River.

Now we turn south toward Ettelbruck, a larger town of almost five thousand people. It is the en-

Luxembourg with its churches and bridges and ruins of old fortifications.

trance to the Ardennes and is an important tourist center. Its picturesque surroundings make it a favorite tourist attraction. Diekirch, to the east, is somewhat smaller and is also a well-known tourist center. We take time out to visit the old church which is well over a thousand years old. The altar, it is said, goes back to pre-Christian days, so it must have been used in pagan worship.

We now turn northward to Vianden, which we have already visited, with its big, old castle. Our impression is the same as it was on our previous visit —Vianden is truly an old, old town. We drive on through the Ardennes highlands, stopping briefly at

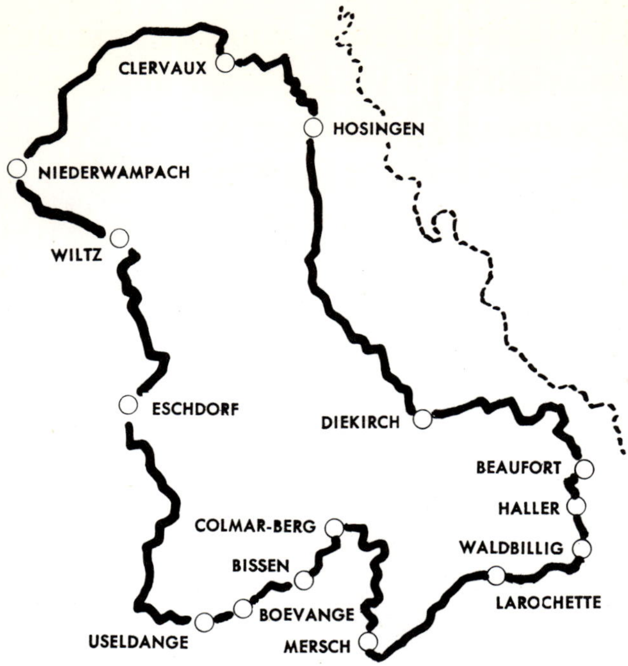

Heinerscheid and Troisvierges. We are now in the extreme north of the Luxembourg Ardennes. Its beautiful parish church is one that will be long remembered.

From Troisvierges it is but a few miles southward to Clervaux, our starting point. Today we covered better than a hundred miles and have seen some wonderful sights. I wonder if I will ever be satisfied again with traveling through the flat prairie lands of our Middle Western states after seeing Luxembourg.

Little Journey No. 5—152 kilometers (94 miles)

There is another road out of Clervaux, I am told, that will take me through some country new to me. Since all Luxembourg roads lead to interesting scenes, I will take this road, winding first north, then west, then south, to a village with the unusual name of Niederwampach. In spite of its very long name, it has only two hundred inhabitants.

Near the village is a war memorial erected by the Belgian people to honor the American soldiers who died in the World War. Again we go through Wiltz, the big castle standing silent and grim above the lower town. We continue southward, soon going through Eschdorf, enjoying again the magnificent view of the Sure Valley below. The Ardennes highlands are always delightful to see!

The road winds on, then turns eastward to Useldange, a village of half a thousand people on the river Attert. A picturesque old castle is visited, its tower dominating the scene. We continue on through the dense woods to Boevange which, like Useldange, is on the Attert River, as is Bissen, which we have visited before. Colmar-Berg, with its summer palace of Grand Duke Jean and his family, is our next stop, a quaint village, about the size of Useldange. Where can all the people of Luxembourg live, we wonder, with so much of the land covered with thick woods?

Winding and twisting, the road goes southward, seldom straight, to Mersch and its big castle among the rolling hills of central Luxembourg. Next we come to Larochette, the picturesque old market town with its two old castles that lie in ruins high above the valley.

Tomb of John the Blind, Luxembourg's national hero.

Several miles out of Larochette the road winds north to the towns of Waldbillig, Haller and Beaufort, each in its own picturesque setting in Moellerdall, Luxembourg's own "Little Switzerland." Here we take time out for a walk in the silent woods, trails leading off in all directions.

Diekirch is our next stop, though we go through the villages of Reisdorf, Moestroff and Bettendorf on the way. We pass the old ninth-century church which we visited several days ago and stop at an inn for a cold drink before going on to Hosingen. We are tempted to stop and take a hike down one of the attractive glens of the Our Valley, but we have already

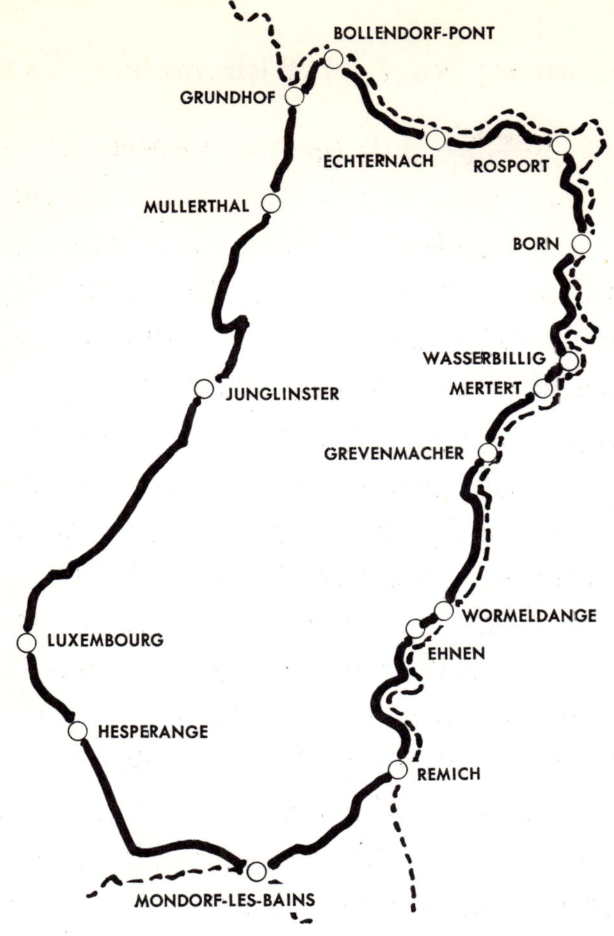

taken one walk in the woods today and decide against another one.

From Hosingen to Clervaux is but a short ride, but the road is winding and speed is impossible. We drive slowly, enjoying the Ardennes woods. Soon we are back in Clervaux, our starting point of this morning, the abbey of St. Maurice towering over the glen. Another day's journey is over; another pleasant day has been spent enjoying fairyland Luxembourg.

Little Journey No. 6—120 kilometers (75 miles)

Today's journey will be the shortest of the eight that we shall take while exploring Luxembourg. When I first arrived in this delightful duchy, I planned to take a one-day trip "to see the country." Now I find myself taking eight, every one pleasant, enjoyable and different from the rest.

We shall start today at Luxembourg City, with its ancient fortifications and its many bridges. We first go to Hamm, just outside the city, where over five thousand American soldiers of the Third Army of General Patton lie buried. Their commander rests with them, a simple cross marking his grave. Close by is a German military cemetery of ten thousand graves, mute testimonies of the waste of war.

From this solemn place we drive northward through rolling hills and green meadows to the village of Junglinster, which has a population of a little less than one thousand. From a distance we see the masts of a radio station and learn upon inquiry that they are the Radio Luxembourg masts, sending out music and other types of programs far and wide. The village is small but old, for there are tombstones of the knights of Linster that have survived the centuries. In nearby Bourglinster is a romantic old manor that is one of the attractions of the region.

To the north is the tiny settlement of Mullerthal, boasting a population of sixty. It is in the "pocket edition" of Switzerland, rough and rugged, with ravines that cut up the land and fantastic rock formations that never cease to inspire awe in those who come to see them. We decide to spend an hour or two walking down a few of the many trails that spread through the region and it proves to be time well spent. Luxembourgers love to walk and they surely have many delightful places in which to do so.

We drive on through similar scenes to Grundhof and Bollendorf-Pont on the Sure River, dividing Luxembourg from Germany. Here we turn southward, following the river to Echternach, which we visited on a previous journey. We are enthralled by the beautiful old houses that line the narrow streets of the town, the roofs and gables steep and slate-covered. How much it looks like a medieval town! It has changed but little through the centuries. The town hall was built almost nine hundred years ago and is still in use, we are told.

As we go southward to Rosport, we enter a region of orchards, the trees heavy with fruit. On the other side of the river is Germany, also with many orchards. We come to Born and continue on, fruit trees on each side of us. At Wasserbillig the Sure and the Moselle rivers join, to continue on to the Rhine. We stop at Mertert for some lunch of delicious sweet rolls and a cold drink. Such a drink, we find, is considerably cheaper than coffee, which sells for two dollars a pound here. All over Europe it is expensive.

Once in East Germany I found that stores were charging eight dollars a pound for it, and not very good coffee at that.

Grevenmacher, a few miles farther on, is a larger town of about three thousand people. We are now in the vine-growing Moselle River Valley. The sparkling wines produced here are known throughout Europe and America for their excellence. Wormeldange and Ehnen are also vine-growing villages on the Moselle, the former with cooperative wine cellars that are huge, like those of Grevenmacher. Remich, too, farther to the south, is surrounded by vineyards and is an important wine center. Its wine cellars are among the attractions of the Moselle Valley.

At Mondorf-les-Baines on the French border are several springs of mineral water, attracting thousands of people each year to "take the cure." The town has delightful parks and we pause long enough to listen to a concert before going on to Hesperance, a peaceful village just three miles from Luxembourg City, our starting point.

Our journey today was pleasant, from beginning to end. What will we remember the longest? The vine-covered slopes of the Moselle Valley? The wine cellars? Medieval Echternach? The orchards of Born? Time alone will tell.

Our next journey will take us to the very southern section of Luxembourg, to the vast steel and iron

mills of Esch on the Alzette River, that have done so much for the welfare of the people.

Little Journey No. 7—160 kilometers (100 miles)

We will begin our drive at the capital city, leaving it still shrouded in morning mists as we take a cross-country road through Hesperange to Remich. As we look back, the higher portions of the city stand out above the mists. The city's one lone skyscraper seems oddly out of place in its surroundings.

From Hesperange to Remich on the Moselle is a pleasant drive, our route taking us through several small villages. The dew is still heavy on the grape vines when we arrive at the vineyards, sparkling in the sun. Just out of Remich we drive through the small villages of Wellenstein and Bech-Kleinmacher nestled among vine-covered hills. The villages are small, but they are important to the wine industry. In Wellenstein are huge wine cellars which we visit.

We continue on through Mondorf-les-Bains on the French border with its hot springs which make it a health resort for ailing people. Bettembourg in the valley of the Alzette is the entrance to the mining district of Luxembourg and we know that we will soon be in Esch-sur-Alzette with its big mills. But first we must visit Dudelange, a town of fifteen thousand people, the tall chimneys of the mills pouring forth smoke. As if to counteract the effects, outdoor swimming pools attracted many persons today. Several towers provide diving boards, the more daring older divers seeking out the taller towers. Everyone seems to enjoy being in the water.

Nearby Kayl is an attractive village of several thousand people, surrounded by wooded hills, a white church tower pointing upward like the finger of God in the center of town. Here is a monument dedicated to the miners who met death in the mines.

From Kayl we take a short drive southward to the town of Rumelange, population between four and five thousand. It proves to be an industrial town and mining center, busy and industrious. After a short visit we return to Kayl and then on to Esch-sur-Alzette, Luxembourg's second largest city. While it

Making steel, a major industry of southern Luxembourg.

is the country's most important industrial town with great steel mills and iron works, it has not neglected beauty, either. In its fine park is a rose garden that is known far and wide. Surrounding the city are vast woods with many paths for hikers. Millions of tons of iron ore are made into more millions of tons of steel and iron products.

From Bettembourg on the east to Rodange on the west, the great industrial center spreads. Here the towns are large: Esch, 29,000; Differdange, 19,000; Dudelange, 15,000; Petange, 8,000; Rodange, 4,200. I am told that 15 percent of the population of Luxembourg live on farms, but the iron and steel industry is the country's most important industry. No fewer than thirty blast furnaces and half that number of steel and rolling mills make Luxembourg one of the eight great steel and iron nations.

At Differdange we ignore the mills and visit the park, which has an unusual flower clock, very pretty to see. A fine stadium provides a place for sports-minded persons to take in events of interest. We drive on to the neighboring towns of Rodange and Petange pleasantly situated at the foot of the Titelberg, the location of ruins that date back to Roman days.

Now we drive northward to Steinfort on the Belgian border and to picturesque Eischen and its church built on a steep hill, to Saeul, an old agricultural village, and to Mersch, which we have also vis-

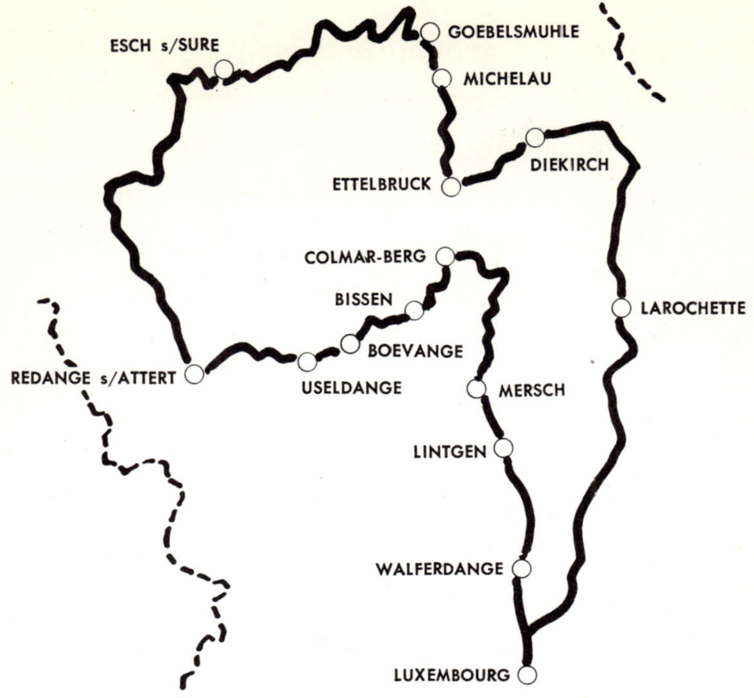

ited before. From here to our starting point is an easy, pleasant drive. So ends our seventh "Little Journey." Only one more left!

Little Journey No. 8— 155 kilometers (96 miles)

While again today we will visit some places that we have previously seen, there will be roads, too, over which we have not yet traveled. Luxembourg has many roads and trails, but by tonight we will have visited most of them.

We will begin our journey at the capital city and drive northward, the bridges over the ravines as wet as if it had rained in the night. Fog and dew can be almost as wet as rain! We go through the quaint old market town of Larochette, the farmers' stalls and tables already filled and ready for customers to come and buy. We do not stop, but go on to bigger Diekirch where a coffee stop is welcome. Since we have already visited the town, we go on to Michelau and Goebelsmuhle in the Ardennes, the latter village's thirty inhabitants all busy with their day's activities.

From here to Esch-sur-Sure the road is a continuous curve as it twists and winds through the rugged country. We are going through the most scenic and picturesque part of Luxembourg and are in no hurry. Although we have previously stopped in Esch, we do so again, to view the steep crags and to marvel at the location of the little village, almost completely surrounded by the Sure River. What a place this would be in which to live! It is no wonder that it is a favorite tourist town. To visit it once means to most certainly come back again, if for no other reason than to check one's memory to see if it is playing tricks. The ruins of the old castle are still there, high above the river and the village.

Reluctantly we go on, loathe to leave the scene of so much beauty. The winding road turns southward, Ardennes scenery on both sides of the road. It is a wonderful drive to Rodange on the Attert River. We think of the Romans of two thousand years ago building a fort on the Titelberg, so far from home and friends. But this won't do; we came to spend an enjoyable day driving about, not to worry about some soldiers of long ago becoming homesick!

We go through Useldange, Boevange and Bissen before we come to Colmar-Berg where Grand Duke Jean's big summer residence stands. There we turn south to Mersch, in the very center of Luxembourg, with its old, old castle, restored after being destroyed. South of Mersch, only a few miles away, is Lintgen, in a hilly, wooded region.

Now we are approaching our starting point, but first a stop must be made at one of the inns for coffee before taking one last walk in the woods. Our little journeys are almost ended. Luxembourg City is now just a couple of miles away. We drive on and soon it is in sight. Our trip is over! It has been one more day crowded with sights and scenes that are now to become memories. Tomorrow we will say "Au Revoir" and leave Luxembourg, so small but so lovely.

Luxembourg, a city of hills and valleys and old, old buildings.

Chapter VII

A VISIT TO LUXEMBOURG CITY

There are few places in the world that are more enjoyable to visit than little Luxembourg—and the heart of the country beats in the capital city of the same name. In picturesque beauty and grandeur of scenery, it will admit being second to none. It is perched on great rocks and towers above the surrounding territory in a magnificent manner.

It is a city of many bridges, for wherever you go, there is a bridge close by. Its narrow streets are crooked, winding among the valleys just as they did long centuries ago. As a visitor nears it from the north, he is greeted with a sight that will be long remembered. There seems to be no level land wherever one looks. Rocky crags and high fortification walls are everywhere. Tall cathedral spires rise into the sky, reflected in the waters of the Alzette River below as it winds through the valley. The city is very, very old, but one need not be told this. It is apparent wherever one looks.

One of Luxembourg City's beautiful parks.

The roofs of the buildings are steep, punctured by countless chimneys and dormers. Many of them are of red tile, though other colors blend in well. Old and careworn, they carry their age well. But there are other buildings, too, as modern as today. Where can one find a more beautiful and up-to-date building than the new theater? Or the international fair building? Or the European center? They do not seem out of place at all, for Luxembourg is both new and old, modern and ancient. In one section, crooked streets wind in and out, lined by buildings that have seen many years. Not far away are streets that are wide and inviting, crowded with pedestrians. It is a city of contrasts, of the unexpected.

One writer who visited Luxembourg called it "a dozen cities in one." Another who visited it said, "It has the poise and pose of Gibraltar, the bridge and spire profile of Bruges, the flowered beauty of Paris, the historical charm of Brussels, and the mystery of a temple city of the Orient. No capital in the world is quite like Luxembourg!"

When one visits the city to see for himself what it is like, he must agree with that writer. It is a medieval town, yet not altogether, for it is very modern in places; it is a centuries-old fortress town, but it is also a twentieth-century city. Wherever one wanders about the town, he strolls down quaint, crooked streets no wider than alleys, then suddenly he comes upon a broad boulevard.

Visitors love to leave the wide avenues to explore inviting side streets that lead to thousand-year-old walls and ramparts, some of which are hewn out of solid rock. A tunnel entrance looms before the visitor, but he hesitates to enter, for there are no less than fourteen miles of underground passageways, built in an era of strife and conflict.

Many are the famous men and women who have come to Luxembourg to see the fabled beauty of the city for themselves. When Louis XIV, most splendid of all the French kings, visited the fortressed city almost three hundred years ago, it was already old

Municipal Theatre—Luxembourg City.

Luxembourg City—a night view.

and seasoned. He was told of one of the Luxembourger's favorite dishes, smoked pork and broad beans. He insisted upon some of it being prepared for his royal person. Upon tasting it, he found it good, and later, upon returning home to France, he requested it often.

A century and a quarter later, Napoleon himself honored the city with a visit. He had not intended to stay more than an hour or two, but so interested was he in the fortifications that three days went by before he could bring himself to leave.

The famous German writer Goethe visited Luxembourg and found it to be enchanting. It was during autumn of the year 1792, when the trees were in their best color and the woods that he loved so well were beautiful.

"This is a spot," he wrote, "where so much grandeur and grace, so much exquisite loveliness are found side by side that one can only wish that Poussin (an outstanding French painter of a century earlier) had seen and painted it."

The English artist Turner visited the city and painted its scenes in watercolor, giving to the future impressions of the beauty of the past. The great fortress is now gone, but the city itself has lost none of its charm.

There were others, too, who came to see and to revel in the city's historic beauty. The great composer Liszt journeyed to Luxembourg to visit a friend, and while there, gave a public concert. It proved to be his last, for he died shortly afterward.

Following the victory over the Germans in 1946, Winston Churchill paid an official visit to the city and was greeted wildly by the grateful people. General Dwight D. Eisenhower, who later became President of the United States, visited the capital city and received a hero's welcome.

Luxembourg today has a population of 80,000 people. It is by far the largest city in the Grand Duchy. There are few industrial plants within its borders to pollute the air and the river water. Green fields and meadows creep right up to the city's edge. Parks and playgrounds abound. Elegant bridges and imposing viaducts span the many ravines and valleys within the city. It is truly a delightful place to visit, with its shops, its churches and its museums. Not many cities have so much to offer to visitors.

Children's dancing procession. This traditional procession dates far back through the years, the origin lost in antiquity.

Chapter VIII

AN OLD, OLD TOWN CALLED ECHTERNACH

On the eastern border where the Sure River separates Luxembourg from its big neighbor, Germany, stands a village of several thousand people. The country round about it is rough and rugged, with strange rock formations and steep cliffs with caves burrowed into their sides. In this "Little Switzerland" is Echternach, a strangely beautiful town as old as the hills that surround it.

Just how old the town is, nobody knows. It stood here already when in the year 698 a monk arrived from Ireland, intent upon reconverting the people of the region to Christianity. Powerful Rome had fallen and many people living along its borders had deserted the religion of Christ, worshipping once again the heathen gods that they had believed in before the Romans came. The monk Willibrord came to

Dancing procession at Echternach, a solemn observance.

save these people from their own folly, to show them the true way to salvation.

To Echternach he came, and there he stayed to build an abbey which bore his name. Willibrord the Benedictine monk became St. Willibrord, patron saint of Echternach. He came to this village to live and here he has remained, though more than eleven centuries have passed since his death. His remains lie in a marble coffin that rests in a crypt of the church built in the year 800.

Echternach is a town that shows its age. Its streets are narrow and crooked, winding this way and that through the town. The buildings that line the streets hold each other up, for if they all stood singly, they would surely fall down.

St. Willibrord was a holy man who did his work well. His mission in life was to restore the faith of the people who had long been deprived of the gospel, and this he did. When he died in 832, after thirty-four years in Echternach, the big abbey that he founded had become known to all of Europe. Many were the miracles that he had performed during his lifetime; now in death the people who loved him were not content to see them cease. They placed his body in a coffin and continued to visit the crypt in which it lay, seeking the help in death that he had so unselfishly given in life. The fame of Willibrord, abbot of Echternach and bishop of Utrecht, spread far and wide beyond the borders of the land that came to be

Dancing procession. A close-up view of the dancers, each one holding onto a handkerchief.

called Luxembourg, into far countries. People who heard began to make pilgrimages to his town, imploring his help. This they do even today. In time, the village became a great religious center.

The basilica, begun in the eighth century, shortly after the death of the saintly man, grew until by the eleventh century it had become one of the finest in northern Europe. The monks who inhabited it made it ever more grand, convinced that the one whom they honored was grateful. In time it became a princely palace, complete with fine gardens and many paths for walking.

Luxembourg City at night.

In 1794, when France was in turmoil and its king and queen were beheaded in the streets of Paris, a great feeling arose in France against religion, and an invading French army entered Luxembourg, driving the monks out of the Echternach abbey. Their library was scattered and the center of learning that had existed for over a thousand years ceased to be. So it is today. The abbey remains, but the monks are gone. Now it is a school attended by Echternach boys and girls.

The pilgrimages that began in the early Middle Ages continue as before. On Whit Tuesday each year, devout people come from all about to take part in as strange a procession as can be found anywhere in Christendom. It is called the "Sprang prozession." As the men, women and children of all ages take part in it, they don't march. They dance a strange sort of dance. They shuffle forward toward one side of the street five steps, then go back three, with the same shuffling motion. This is done to music played by band instruments of many kinds, violins, flutes, guitars, stringed instruments and wind instruments. Even brass pieces are used, playing a strange, haunting tune over and over again as those in the parade advance and retreat, their progress maddeningly slow. At the head of the procession are the priests, followed by the children. Then come the older boys and girls and finally the men and women, all shuffling, shuffling, each one holding in his hand the corner of a handkerchief, the opposite corner held by the person next to him. They are from Echternach and from the towns and villages about it.

The parade begins early in the morning and continues throughout the day, hour after hour, down the cobbled streets to St. Willibrord's tomb in the abbey that he founded. It is in his honor that the strange procession is held, to invoke his blessing.

When did this unusual observance begin? No one knows, though it was mentioned already in records of the eighth century. Why is it held? There are those who say that nobody knows. Others there are who aver that it is to invoke St. Willibrord's help

Remembrance Day, Ettelbruck. The people of Luxembourg are a freedom-loving people and they resent greatly the attempts of their German neighbors to take over their country.

against epilepsy. Long ago, when he was alive, he cured children suffering from the disease by touching them with his hand. In death, what could believing parents do but carry their ailing children to his tomb, to seek his blessing and a cure?

Historians and scholars have searched the records but have failed to find the answer. And so the unusual ceremony continues year after year, those taking part being very serious and firm in their faith that only good can come from their way of honoring the patron saint of the city. Surely such a strange thing as this parade could happen only in the old, old town of Echternach.

Chapter IX

THE CASTLES OF LUXEMBOURG

When a popular American magazine carried an article which stated that there are a hundred and twenty-eight castles in Luxembourg, it was promptly corrected by an authority on the subject.

"There are a hundred and thirty-eight castles in Luxembourg," he stated.

Which figure is correct is really not important. A visitor would probably lose all interest in castles after viewing a baker's dozen of them. I am content with the knowledge that I have seen quite a few of them even though I know that there are many more to be seen. That is the reason why Luxembourg is called "The Land of the Haunted Castles."

The nobles of the Middle Ages made strong fortifications of their homes, which served as both castle and strong fort or fortress. Around each one were clustered the peasants' farms, each household looking to the nobleman for protection in times of trouble. In time, almost every locality had a castle of

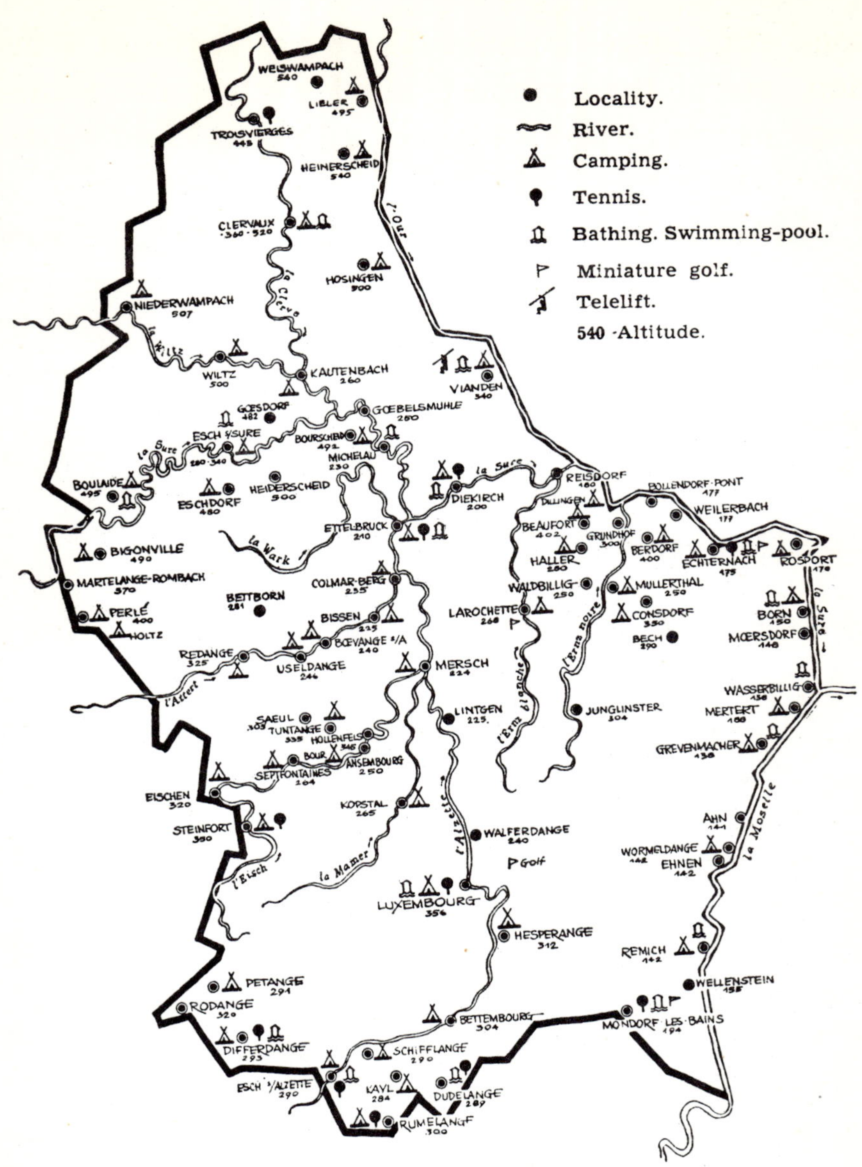

LET'S GO CAMPING!

"The Land of Haunted Castles" is a wonderful place to go camping. Most of the year the climate is ideal and many campgrounds are provided. Campers can spend several weeks in Luxembourg at very little cost. They will always find other campers in the campgrounds, often leading to lasting friendships.

some sort, large or small. The great castle of Vianden, one of the grandest of all west of the Rhine, once served as protection for a hundred and thirty-six villages round about it.

Luxembourg has more than its share of castles because of its strategic position between France and Germany. It has seen invaders come and go from the time of the Romans when Caesar's legions marched northward to conquer the German tribes—a goal that was never achieved. From that time to the year that Hitler's panzers crossed the Moselle into Luxembourg, the region was seldom free from invasion or the fear of it. Small wonder that so many strong castles were built!

A rugged terrain and forested land cut up by steep valleys, some five hundred feet deep, a few even a thousand feet, provided a natural setting for the castles. A village would begin to grow at the foot of a steep hill. In time a wall would be built around it to protect it from wandering marauders. On the top of the hill a castle would then be built. Round towers and strong battlements were typical features of these castles.

So like one's idea of fairyland are most Luxembourg scenes that on more than one occasion I thought, "This whole land could have been dreamed up by Walt Disney!" I wonder if Walt Disney ever saw Luxembourg? It would have been an inspiration to him! And what is more natural than that folktales and fairy tales should "grow up" in such a beautiful and fantastic land?

In days of old, knights in armor played a leading role in the life of Luxembourg. They fought each other as willingly as they fought invaders from other lands. Their homes, the big, cold, cheerless castles, were not as comfortable as our homes are today and there were few pastimes to while away the days. Perhaps that is why the knights quarreled and fought so much—there was little else to do!

Clervaux, like Vianden, has a famous castle, huge in size. It was once the home of the De Lannoi family. Philip De Lannoi left for America in the seventeenth century and settled in New England. It is possible that he may be one of Franklin Delano Roosevelt's ancestors, the "De Lannoi" being changed in time to "Delano."

Other castles are found at Beaufort and Schoenfels, at Bourglinster and Bourscheid, at Mersch—and at a hundred other places in Luxembourg, some still in use, some in ruins. "The Land of Haunted Castles" is a wonderful place to visit!

Chapter X

RADIO LUXEMBOURG

The site where Radio Luxembourg now stands was once a part of the city's vast ring of forts. The sound that comes from it booms out to all of Europe, greater than the roar of cannon that once issued forth.

Radio Luxembourg is without doubt the noisiest, brassiest station on the continent. The city and the country are so quiet and peaceful that it is hard to understand why the radio station should be so different.

It is remarkable in other ways, too. Its power is tremendous, the main transmitter being 600,000 watts strong. Its message, often consisting of rock music, is carried throughout the countries of Europe, into North Africa, and far into the communist Soviet Union. Unbelievably, it broadcasts in eleven different languages!

Rock formations in the neighborhood of Berdorf.

"This is 'Radio Lucky Luxembourg,' " calls out the cheerful English-speaking disc jockey to his many listeners.

This radio station has made the name of Luxembourg famous throughout all of Europe. The country may be small but its enterprises are great. Once it had the strongest fortress in Europe; now it has the most powerful radio station.

During World War II this station was used to broadcast Nazi propaganda, much to the disgust of the people of the conquered country. The English traitor William Joyce, who was better known as Lord Haw Haw, was vicious in his broadcasts. When Germany was defeated, Joyce was captured and returned to England. He was tried for treason, convicted and hanged.

One day while riding in a bus alongside the Moselle River which forms Luxembourg's eastern boundary, I was surprised to hear the voice of a radio announcer peal forth in English.

"This is Radio Lucky Luxembourg!" he said. "You will now hear that favorite of so many people, 'Danny Boy.' "

This selection had long been a favorite song of mine and I had heard it in many places, but I never expected to hear it in a bus in the heart of Europe.

Since then I have heard Radio Luxembourg in many cities; in Lucerne, Switzerland; in Nuremburg, Germany; in tiny Monaco on the Mediterranean; in

Copenhagen and Paris and Brussels. Certainly it is one of the busiest radio stations in all Europe.

How does it happen that this station is such a popular one? Certainly there are not enough sponsors in this small country to support such a powerful and expensive station. That is right; there are not. It is foreign firms that support this station, advertising their wares on the air. Radio Luxembourg has a wide audience throughout Europe, principally for the reason that most radio stations of that continent are controlled by the various governments. As such, they cannot broadcast freely but are limited to only such matters as the government approves. Radio Luxembourg is one of the few big "free" stations, broadcasting what it chooses.

Chapter XI

A STORY OF A BRAVE SOLDIER

A year or two ago there was a very popular movie being shown in American theaters. It was called "Patton" and it was the story of a very famous American general who helped to defeat the Germans in 1945.

The war was almost over when the German army made a last desperate attempt at victory. It failed, thanks to many brave soldiers and to an American general named George S. Patton. It was he who commanded the Third Army that stopped the Germans in their tracks and drove them back.

General Patton is buried in the big military cemetery at Hamm, a suburb just outside the city of Luxembourg. There are thousands of crosses in the Hamm cemetery, plain white crosses, each one marking the grave of an American soldier who died in battle. One of the crosses stands just a little apart from the others, though it is simple and plain like the rest of them. It is that of General Patton, who died

Hamm, U. S. military cemetery and General George S. Patton's burial place.

not in battle, but in an automobile accident seven months after the war ended.

Near a little village not far from the Belgian border is the grave of another American soldier. His name was George Ottmar Mergenthaler and he was the grandson of Ottmar Mergenthaler whose life story is found in the book of famous Americans called "Famous Americans Born Abroad." He was the inventor of the Linotype machine.

George was the only son of a wealthy New York couple. Although his grandfather had been born in Germany, George had returned there in World War II as a soldier in the United States Army, intent upon helping to defeat Hitler's troops. He was a member of the 28th Division which had landed in Normandy and had fought its way across France. The American soldiers were weary, but it seemed to them that the war was nearing its end, for the Germans were in retreat.

George Mergenthaler was glad, too, for he was tired of fighting and looked forward to going home again. In November 1944, he was in the village of Eschweiler in Luxembourg near the Belgian border, assigned to stay at the home of the local priest, Father Antoine Bodson. The two became good friends, for the priest spoke English and George was 24, Princeton educated, friendly, and able to speak some German.

But let Father Bodson tell the story.

"George Mergenthaler and I spent more than a month together," he said. "We became very good friends. Each evening we spent together, listening to music and to the radio, which told us of the progress of the war. We both felt that the terrible war was about over and looked forward to the return of peace."

Father Bodson stopped, and his thoughts went back to the events of a quarter of a century ago. He continued his story.

"The Christmas season arrived. George had received several packages from home, but the Christmas package was his favorite for it contained a very attractive vest which he wore under his army uniform. He was very proud of his fine vest and wore it every day."

Through the months during which George Mergenthaler was stationed in Eschweiler he had become well acquainted with the local people, who liked him very much. He seemed happy to talk to anyone who had the time to talk with him, and most people did. He was interested in them, in their work, in their everyday affairs.

"Herr Mergenthaler is very nice," they would say to each other, for Mr. Mergenthaler was indeed a favorite with everyone.

December 16, 1944, was a tragic day for the people of the Ardennes region. On that day the rumble of guns was again heard. The Battle of the Bulge had begun; the Germans were coming back. On the morning of that day George Mergenthaler went to mass and reassured the frightened people.

"We will take care of them," he promised. "Never fear."

But the battle developed into more of a fight than he and the other Americans expected. Many Nazi divisions were sent against them in an attempt to break through and overrun France. There were more than 350,000 desperate German soldiers involved. They did not succeed in breaking the American line, but they did make a huge bulge in it. Ever afterward this phase of the war was known as the Battle of the

Bulge. Twenty thousand Americans were killed during the following several weeks, with countless thousands more wounded in the terrible fighting.

When the German tanks began to appear on the road that led from Eschweiler to Bastogne, George Mergenthaler dug himself a foxhole back a bit from the road and prepared to do what he could to stop their advance. That was the last time that the villagers saw their American friend.

Christmas came and went; the cold of January settled over the Ardennes. Before February arrived, the invaders had been driven back and the villagers who had fled the Nazi advance returned to their homes. But George Mergenthaler did not return, and his friends in Eschweiler feared for his safety. Many of their homes had been destroyed; Father Bodson's church was in ruins. But George did not return. Perhaps he had been captured, the people hoped, but they held their fears to themselves. Thousands of young American men would never return to their homes across the ocean, they knew, because of the events of the weeks just passed.

When spring came, some villagers found a shallow grave in the meadow just outside of town. A crude cross marked the site; a GI's helmet hung from the cross. Father Bodson hastened to the spot and removed some stones from the crude grave. Beneath them was the body of a man; his American uniform was still recognizable. Beneath it was the vest that George Mergenthaler had received from America just before the Germans returned. There was no doubt about it. It was here in his foxhole that their American friend had died, determined that the enemy should not pass.

"I knew that it was my friend George," wrote Father Bodson to the young soldier's parents in America. "I am a man who is used to coming face to face with death, but I could not keep back the grief that overcame me at that moment. I wept."

Two days later, as the Angelus sounded over the village, the young man was buried in the church cemetery. All the people of the village were present. A marker was later put on the spot where the body was found in the foxhole alongside the road that led to Bastogne.

Father Bodson's church has been repaired and a new organ has been bought, in part with money sent by George Mergenthaler's parents. Behind the altar is a mural, painted by a local artist. In it, Christ is seated among his followers, who listen as he speaks to them. Beside him stands a robed figure—it is a likeness of the young American who chose to die defending the homes of the villagers whom he loved. Each time the people attend mass, they are reminded of this brave soldier who came three thousand miles to die and who will spend eternity with them.

Chapter XII

HOW LUXEMBOURG IS GOVERNED

When I told a class of young people that Luxembourg is a democracy, just as the United States is, one of the students asked, "But how can it be a democracy when it has a grand duke at its head? Isn't a grand duke about the same as a king?"

It is true that a grand duke "reigns" in Luxembourg, but he does not "rule." Some countries even have kings or queens, but they have little real power, such as England, for example. Queen Elizabeth II does no real "ruling." On the other hand, East Germany is called a "Peoples' Democratic Republic," but the people have no real voice in their government. A dictator and his chosen clique do all of the governing. One must not be misled by a name.

In Luxembourg, the legislative power is held by the Chamber of Deputies. That is, it makes the laws. There are fifty-six representatives in the Chamber

A candidate for public office speaks to a group of listeners.

of Deputies. This body of delegates corresponds to our House of Representatives. The members are elected by the people of Luxembourg, just as they are here.

The executive power rests in the hands of the grand duke and a cabinet. The president of the council is selected from the group and is appointed by the grand duke. The council discusses proposed laws and deliberates on matters of concern. They give their opinions on matters of state to the grand duke. It is their duty to advise him.

In our country, there are two major parties, the Republican and the Democratic. Little Luxembourg has five parties, though only three can be called major parties. In a recent election, twenty-two elected members were "Christian-Socialists"; twenty-one were "Socialists"; six were "Democrats" and five were "Communists." A new party appeared at this election, the "Independent Popular Movement," but it elected only two members.

When no party has a majority in the Chamber of Deputies, it is necessary for the several parties to form a "coalition government," in which case representatives of the various parties combine and work together. Naturally, the parties having the most elected members also have the most power in the Chamber of Deputies.

Committees are appointed and discussions take place just as they do in our own government in Washington or in the various state governments.

The sovereign of Luxembourg reigns for life unless he or she resigns. In 1964, the Grand Duchess Charlotte, after a reign of forty-five years, resigned and her son, Grand Duke Jean, became the head of state. He took the oath of office on November 12, 1964. He is married and has five children: Prince Henri, Prince Jean, Prince Guillaume, Princess Marie-Astrid and Princess Margaretha.

Grand Duke Jean was born at the royal castle in Berg, Luxembourg, on January 5, 1921. He received his elementary and secondary education in Luxembourg and attended college in England. While exiled from his country during World War II, he studied law and political science at Laval University in Quebec, Canada.

Grand Duke Jean is popular with the people of his country. He is a democratic monarch, content to have his subjects make the laws under which they all live.

Chapter XIII

EDUCATION AND ART

The people of the duchy are quick to point out to visitors that all of them can read and write. This can be said of few countries.

It was not always true of Luxembourg either. During the Middle Ages ignorance prevailed everywhere in Europe. Even many of the lords and other nobles of the various countries were unable to read and write. The church alone kept the flame of learning burning, though for centuries it flickered feebly.

The monks in their monasteries spent endless hours copying by hand old books of learning. Some of these beautiful books are still in existence, mute evidence of the devotion expended upon each of them.

Learning remained at a low level throughout Luxembourg until the country achieved its independence in 1815. Then a new national spirit arose and developed. Schools were established and the education of children became general. Today their

Education in Luxembourg takes many forms. Here a student is being trained in skillful pottery making.

goals have been achieved—everyone in the country who is educable can read and write.

Children attend school in Luxembourg even as they do in America, although education there is much more formal than it is here. There is not the freedom in the classroom that we have nor is the subject matter taught as broad or as varied. The usual subjects such as reading, writing and arithmetic get the greatest attention, though geography, science and other subjects are also taught.

Restricted in size and limited in resources, Luxembourg is doing its best to educate its young people in a practical manner. Vocational courses are being emphasized more and more in the secondary schools.

The same problems that plague other countries are found here, such as a trend toward leaving the villages and farms on the part of the younger people. What this will eventually do to the country, time alone can tell.

Luxembourg is trying hard to keep pace with a fast-changing world. It is well placed, tucked among larger nations. Traditionally, the people are conservative, not inclined to rapid changes. Its national motto tells us much about the people and their attitudes: "We wish to remain what we are." In the past they have been overrun by foreign armies and ruled by first one nation, then another. During the lifetime of its older citizens, it has been twice invaded and terrorized. Now it is a member of the Common Market, the United Nations, NATO and other progressive organizations, taking its place in the modern world.

In the field of literature, Luxembourg has no authors who have become prominent beyond its own borders. Its small size alone may account for this, for a nation of a third of a million people can hardly expect to produce outstanding authors to compete with those of nations of fifty or a hundred million population.

Yet the country does possess a literature of its own. Fiction, plays and poetry written in the national language are published regularly. Perhaps the greatest literary production by a native of the country is the long poem entitled "Reynard the Fox." It was written by Michael Rodange, who lived from 1827 to 1867, dying at the early age of forty. In addition to works of poetry and fiction, historical writings are a favorite. Also, a national folklore has developed that is typically Luxembourgian.

Modern art has gone forward with great strides during the present century. The members of the artistic "Cercle Artistique," which was founded in 1893, have done much to develop modern art in the country. Liez and Fresez were two outstanding nineteenth-century artists. Joseph Kutter (1894-1941) ranked among the distinguished artists of Europe. His paintings have been exhibited in the leading art galleries of Paris, Berlin, Brussels and other European art centers. They have also been shown in New York. His early death in 1941 ended a career that promised to extend to even greater heights.

Several institutions of culture deserve mention. The Grand Ducal Institute, founded in 1868, has encouraged research in the fields of history and science. The National Museum in Luxembourg City has on display countless objects of historic interest concerning the duchy. To indicate the long history of Luxembourg, the exhibits are grouped under five main divisions: Prehistoric, Celtic, Roman, Frankish, and Medieval. The National Library houses over 600,000 volumes in addition to many rare old manuscripts.

The Michael Rodange Memorial on the Place Guillaume in the capital city is a tribute to the author of "Reynard the Fox."

The big Radio Luxembourg orchestra deserves mention also. Although the station sometimes favors popular "rock" music, the orchestra frequently broadcasts classical music that is heard by millions of listeners.

It is interesting to note that the church bells of Luxembourg are silent from Good Friday to Easter Sunday. According to folklore, they have flown to Rome to confess! So, the children take over on those days, making the rounds and ringing hand bells to call the people to morning church service.

Another day that the children love is Candlemas, a church festival held on February 2. Candles are blessed in honor of the infant Jesus who was presented in the temple on this day, according to tradition. The Luxembourg children go about on this day carrying candles and singing songs, collecting candy, nuts and fruit as a reward.

There are movies in Luxembourg, just as there are in our country, and playgrounds for the children as well as tennis courts and golf courses for both young and old. A fine stadium has been built in the capital city for football and other athletic events. Baseball has not "caught on" as yet in Luxembourg, nor has England's favorite game of cricket.

Bicycling is a favorite sport in the duchy and on several occasions Luxembourgers have won Europe's greatest long-distance bicycle race, the "Tour de France." Hiking is also popular, and the lovely Luxembourg woods have many beautiful foot trails. Swimming and canoeing are among the most popular outdoor sports, but there are also many places for fishermen and hunters to indulge their favorite pastimes.

There are so many things to do in Luxembourg that no one, whether young or old, need ever be bored. As one goes about the country, he becomes quite sure that very few people are ever bored. They are active and energetic, filled with a strong attachment for their little country.

Chapter XIV

A VISIT TO AN AMERICAN-LUXEMBOURGER

I met my first Luxembourger years ago when I was a child of six or seven. It was on a Saturday, so there was no school in the small Minnesota town in which I lived. In a main-street blacksmith shop, two big men were hard at work at a forge. Sparks were flying as the bellows were pumped. One of the men poked a big piece of iron in the glowing coals, heating it until it was white hot. Then he took it out and held it on an anvil while the other man hammered it with a huge hammer. Repeatedly this was done, and each time it came closer to being the shape that they wanted. A friend and I stood at the shop door, fascinated by what we saw.

As the men worked, intent upon the job that they were doing, they spoke to each other in a language that sounded very strange to me. It wasn't German and it wasn't Dutch, nor was it "Plattdeutsch" or

Sausage products, a food that is very popular in Luxembourg.

Low German. My parents spoke German fluently, so I knew the language well.

"We are Americans, living in America," my parents had once told me. "English is our language." So although they could speak German, English was always used in our home.

Low German was frequently heard on the streets and I recognized it when I heard it. Most of the Hollanders in the town were new arrivals and they still spoke the language of their native country. Therefore, I was puzzled by the tongue of the two big men and asked the boy who was with me what they were speaking. He was two years older than I and so was more worldly wise. Besides, he lived next door to one of the men who were so busy creating something out of a piece of iron at the forge.

"They are talking Luxembourger," he said knowingly. "They're Luxembourgers, you know."

Many years passed. The two big men who had been at the forge that day had long since been at rest in the village cemetery. So were most of the villagers who were grown up when I was a boy looking in on the blacksmith shop happenings that summer day. I returned to my home village after these many years and sought out the son of one of the men. His name was Eugene Thein and he had retired from active work and now lived alone in a big house on a side street. He told me many things about the little country from which his grandfather had come.

"My grandfather, John Peter Thein, came from Luxembourg to America in the year 1845," he said. "Conditions were not good over there at that time. Most of the people lived on small farms and the soil was poor. There was little industry in Luxembourg then, no big steel mills to give work to the people. My ancestors were farmers, though for several generations they were also blacksmiths."

Mr. Thein paused in his story and opened the drawer of a desk that stood nearby. From it he took a strange looking tool resembling a pair of pliers.

"This is a forceps that my grandfather made before the Civil War," he said. "It was used to pull teeth. He made many such tools that were used for special purposes."

He handed me the tool that was now well over a hundred years old. He was proud of his grandfather's ability to do such fine work.

"My grandfather built a blacksmith shop in what was then the village of St. Paul," he continued. "It was located at the foot of what is today the big Robert Street bridge that crosses the Mississippi River. There was no bridge, then; only a ferryboat. His son, Eugene, left St. Paul to live in Clara City. There were other Luxembourgers in this little prairie town: the Schaacks, the Strauses, the Schumans, Thomas, Freilingers, Dondelingers and others. Many of their grandchildren still live around here.

"John Peter Thein's son, Eugene, was my father. He was a blacksmith like his father. My name is Eugene and so is my son's. We keep in touch with the old country. My brother Peter is visiting in Luxembourg now."

So the ties that were broken with the parent country long ago are still being renewed, more than a century later.

I recalled an incident that took place in Germany several years before. There I met a young man by the name of Peter Thein, resident of a small town in Bavaria. I asked Eugene if Peter was, by chance, related to him, but he thought it unlikely.

"Germany has never had much appeal to Luxembourgers," he admitted. "We were afraid that it was always ready to gobble us up, to swallow us as it did in 1914 and again in 1940. When Luxembourgers left their country to live elsewhere, most of them went to America. We looked upon it as a land of freedom and of great opportunity."

Eugene Thein did not say so, but it is well known among the people of the village where he lives that this country has been good to the family. They regard the Theins as wealthy people, for they have been industrious and enterprising, engaging in many activities. Years ago Eugene's father was a well driller. Eugene himself operated a threshing service; his brothers were prominent farm equipment dealers. That their hard work paid off, there is little doubt.

Many families now living in this community whose ancestors came from Luxembourg have remained farmers, tilling the rich soil of western Minnesota. Others are business and professional men. Whatever they turn their hands to, they seem to do well. It is a trait that Luxembourgers have.

Another man told of the difficulties that he met when he first came to America.

"I could speak no English, so I spoke German, which was much more common in this country," he said. "I went into a restaurant one day and seated myself at the counter. When the waitress came, I said, 'Wie gehts?' which means 'How are you?' She didn't understand me and thought that I said 'wheat cakes.'

"When I heard her call out the order to the cook in the kitchen, I cried out, 'Nein! Nein!' (No! No!) Again she misunderstood and brought me NINE big pancakes, a stack six inches high, and I had to pay for three breakfasts!"

Chapter XV

RELIGION IN LUXEMBOURG

In all of Luxembourg, I was told, there is only one Protestant minister. There is also one lone Jewish rabbi, the same official said. It isn't because the people of the country are not religious, for they are. They are devoutly faithful, the vast majority of them belonging to the Roman Catholic church.

When Martin Luther began the reformation of the church, the people of northern Europe followed him by the millions. The Luxembourgers, however, chose to keep the religion of their forefathers, as they have done to this day.

When traveling in Luxembourg, whenever I approached a village, it was the church steeple that stood out prominently. The usual village consists of some simple homes clustered about a church, which generally stands on the highest spot in town.

I approached a village late one afternoon when the sun was low in the sky. A narrow road ran from

The Catholic religion prevails in Luxembourg. Almost every city and hamlet has a beautiful church, its spires pointing skyward.

the low meadows upward, for the village stood on a hill. At the very top of the rise stood a church, old and imposing. It was there when the Americans fought England to gain their independence, as it had been when the Pilgrims first came to our shores. Yes, and it was there when bold Columbus left Spain to sail into the unknown. For hundreds of years it had been there, as solid as the faith in which the villagers believed.

In the early morning, I left the inn and walked up the single street of the town that led to the church. It was cobbled, worn smooth by the shoes of many people. Behind the church was the cemetery, many of the tombstones so old that they were crumbling into dust. Below me the countryside was buried in white fog, only here and there a crag or a tall tree penetrating it. How eerie was the sight of the valley that early morning!

Through the fog came the sound of the church bell, its low tones muffled by the heavy mist, calling the people to early mass. Up the street a few early worshipers slowly made their way, some of them elderly couples who had walked that steep road for so many years.

All over Luxembourg the same thing was happening that morning, as it had for countless mornings in the past and as it would continue to far into the future. Faith and tradition are not easily broken in Luxembourg.

Luxembourg City has a population of 80,000 people, which is not very large as cities go. There are many such places in Europe, but Luxembourg has a distinction all its own. It is a nation's capital and a cathedral town as well, the religious center of the country. The cathedral is the Church of Our Lady of Luxembourg. On holy days, people from all over the country come to worship. Religion to these people is a deeply felt emotion.

The church itself is an imposing structure, half old and half new. The old part of it is a splendid example of architecture of the Middle Ages. The other portion is newer, with magnificent stained glass windows.

When St. Willibrord came to Echternach in the year 698, he came because the people of the region who long ago had become Christians, had fallen away and were worshiping heathen gods. Religion in Luxembourg is almost as old as Christianity itself.

Chapter XVI

A NEW ERA

When Belgium took from helpless Luxembourg half of her territory in 1839, the Treaty of London guaranteed that thereafter the unfortunate little nation's rights would be respected. Its neutrality would be observed and no further land demands by neighboring nations would be permitted.

This policy of neutrality continued for a hundred and one years. Then on May 10, 1940, a change occurred. On that day Luxembourg took its position alongside other European nations, abolishing the neutral position of the country. By this action it became a member of the community of nations, fully grown up.

Mr. Joseph Bech, foreign minister of Luxembourg and venerable statesman of the Grand Duchy, declared to the Chamber of Deputies members, "Our country now understands that it can no longer remain in a position of isolation, which never was splendid. All hope of remaining on such a status has

The iron and steel industry has brought a new prosperity to the Grand Duchy.

now vanished. The events of 1940 (invasion by Germans) have made us, whether we want it or not, very modest participants. We are no longer indifferent, neutral spectators, but actors.

"Our part, I might say, our mission, has been marked out for us by our real interest, which is the solidarity of nations in world affairs and particularly in the European field. This solidarity alone can enable the old continent, if not to reconquer its secular, political and material supremacy, at least to assure its security and liberty with its prosperity, thereby preventing the nations of Europe from sliding toward the abyss."

Textile factories abound, helping the new era to flourish.

Today Luxembourg is an active member of the European group. It has signed the Benelux Agreements (**Be**lgium, **Ne**therlands, **Lux**embourg) and is a member of the North Atlantic Treaty group, the Common Market and the United Nations.

A growing friendship toward the United States and Great Britain on the part of Luxembourg has caused those two nations to appoint ambassadors to the Grand Duchy.

For many years it has been the dream of some people to create a "United Europe," a superstate of nations, just as the United States is one nation composed of many states. This dream remains a vivid one with many Luxembourgers, though they realize that it may be a long time in coming. Language barriers are real, as are religious differences and racial prejudices. Nations, small and large, are proud of their national heritages and do not want to give them up. For these reasons, a "United Europe" will be far more difficult to achieve than a "United States." But hope remains strong in the hearts of many people.

Still and all, Luxembourg, long regarded as a small, unimportant state, has now assumed a position alongside the larger nations of the continent, taking full part in the political and economic movements of Europe. It, too, looks forward to a federation of nations, which many confidently expect to come some day.

In the capital city of Luxembourg is one lone skyscraper, twenty-two stories high, seemingly out of place in the thousand-year-old town. It houses the offices of the European Economic Community and other international organizations. It is a constant reminder to the people that their years of isolation are over, that their country, though small, has now assumed its place in the family of nations. Luxembourg is "going modern," in spite of its old castles and rural character.

Chapter XVII

SOCIAL PROGRESS

In America we have become used to upheavals of one kind or another. Strikes are frequent and labor disputes are everyday occurrences. In this way, some people say, progress is made, slowly but surely. Our country is big and young, so it is natural that it suffers "growing pains" in the process of growing up.

Luxembourg, on the other hand, is small and old. Its social progress has come about slowly and gradually, a step at a time. Because this growth has been steady, it has resulted in significant advances being made without the country being shaken by the social conflicts that have afflicted many countries. In a large measure this has been due to the farsighted policy of the government. One writer has said, "Luxembourg is an oasis of calm and courtesy." Another has called it "a paradise in a nutshell."

Conveyor in dairy plant. Unemployment is almost unknown in Luxembourg.

There are ample reasons for such words of praise. Among the matters with which social legislation has concerned itself in Luxembourg are these:

- Health and accident insurance that covers labor against risks incurred in connection with its jobs.
- Unemployment insurance.
- Sickness insurance.
- Medical assistance.
- Old age pensions.
- Disability pensions.
- The establishment of an eight-hour workday.
- Setting up workers' grievance committees.
- Securing paid holidays for workers.
- Forbidding employment of juveniles under 14 years of age.
- Eliminating night work for women and adolescents.
- Establishing apprentice schools.
- Setting up vocational guidance offices.
- Providing assistance for expectant mothers and nursing care for new mothers.

In addition to these advances, the big steel companies, the largest employers in Luxembourg, have on their own initiative made significant privately sponsored advances. Included among their projects are:

- The establishment of technical schools and colleges.
- Setting up scholarships for promising students.

Tobacco processing and packaging.

- Building houses for employees.
- Providing adequate housing for aged former employees.
- Maintaining hospitals for workers and retirees.
- Providing social aid services.
- Building and maintaining antitubercular preventoria for children.

In other ways, the government has taken the lead in advancing the lot of labor. A fair minimum wage has been established, guaranteeing to every worker, man or woman, a sensible salary. Convalescent centers have been set up for ill workers and health re-

These girls are sorting tobacco leaves which will be made into cigarettes, most of which will be exported.

sorts have been established. All civil servants and government employees are now covered by health insurance.

The objective of these measures has been real social security, which has now become an actuality in the Grand Duchy. Pensions have gradually become higher until now retired workers need no longer fear a dependent old age. As the cost of living rises, adjustments are made. A practice that has not been adopted in the United States but is in effect in Luxembourg is the payment of a fixed sum for every baby born in a family.

Also of significance is the inclusion of all agricultural workers in the social security program. This is of importance since Luxembourg is still an essentially rural country.

The Luxembourg people and their government are proud of the advances that have been made.

Chapter XVIII

SOME IMPORTANT DATES AND EVENTS

58-51 B.C.—Romans invade and conquer lands that are now France and Luxembourg, conquering as far as the Rhine River.

A.D. 250—Goths, Franks and Alemanni tribes invade Luxembourg. Many settle in the Moselle Valley.

406-433—Repeated invasion by Franks, Burgundians and Huns.

882—Normans (Northmen) invade and conquer.

963—Siegfried (Sigefroid) acquires Lucilinburhuc (Luxembourg) Rock.

1083—Conrad I, Count of Luxembourg, founds Benedictine abbey near his castle.

1200-1252—The towns of Echternach, Thionville, Luxembourg and Grevenmacher receive charters. Vigorous development of monastic life; many holy orders establish monasteries.

Grand Duke Jean, present ruler of Luxembourg.

1270—Henry V of Luxembourg and Louis of France go on a crusade to the Holy Land.

1288, June 5—Henry VI and three of his brothers die in the Battle of Worringen near Cologne.

1308—Henry of Luxembourg becomes emperor of the Holy Roman Empire.

1310-1346—Reign of John the Blind. On August 26, 1346, he was killed in the Battle of Crecy while fighting against the English.

1354—Luxembourg becomes a duchy.

1443—The Burgundians take over Luxembourg.

1445—Philip the Good sets up a council to assist in governing the duchy.

1479—The French lay siege to Luxembourg town.

1509—The town of Luxembourg is swept by fire.

1554—A gunpowder explosion and fire destroy much of the town.

1564—A revolt against Spain begins.

1550-1600—Witchcraft trials spread in Luxembourg.

1593-1609—The Duchy of Luxembourg is raided repeatedly by Dutch mercenaries.

1603—Jesuit College opens its doors in the town of Luxembourg.

1613—Construction of the Jesuit Church, now the Luxembourg Cathedral, begins.

1627—The first nuns of the congregation of Our Lady take over the education of girls.

1635—Throughout this century, Luxembourg is looted by troops of several countries. Famines and epidemics depopulate the country.

1684—The French conquer Luxembourg, though in 1698 it is again given to Spain.

1713—Luxembourg is given to the Hapsburgs of Austria.

1735—Large-scale fortifications are begun that make the city of Luxembourg the strongest in central Europe.

1789—The peasants of the Ardennes revolt. The uprising is put down with great cruelty.

1794-95—Luxembourg is captured and comes under the control of the French.

1804, October—Napoleon Bonaparte visits Luxembourg. Thousands of young men join his army.

1815—The Grand Duchy of Luxembourg becomes a sovereign state and a member of the German Confederation.

1839—The Duchy is split in two, the western half of the country becoming a part of Belgium. Modern Luxembourg evolves out of the remains.

1860-1890—An industrial revolution spreads over southern Luxembourg, centering about the iron and steel industry.

1868-1878—The great fortifications of the city of Luxembourg are demolished.

1914-1918—World War I. German troops violate Luxembourg's neutrality and occupy the country.

1919—After the defeat of Germany, the people of Luxembourg hold a referendum. They approve the monarchy, as of old. The constitution provides for woman suffrage and proportional representation in the Chamber of Deputies.

1926—Luxembourg is admitted to the League of Nations.

1940—German troops again occupy the Grand Duchy of Luxembourg and hold it by force for four years.

1946—Luxembourg again freed.

Chapter XIX

A BRIEF LOOK AT WHAT WE HAVE LEARNED

We have learned many interesting and sometimes surprising things about Luxembourg. It is a tiny country, about the size of many American counties, with a population of about a third of a million people. French is the official language, but most newspapers are printed in German. However, the people speak Luxembourger or "Letzeburgesch," which is a folk dialect.

The northern and western half of the country is rough and rugged, known as the Ardennes highland region. Here the land is forested and cut up by many streams. The people call this the E'sleck.

The southern portion is a plains region, more suited to agriculture, where potatoes and grains grow well. Along the Moselle River which divides Luxembourg from Germany, grapes are grown which are made into wine and champagne. In the extreme

The royal family and their five children. Seated from left to right they are Princess Marie-Astrid, Princess Margaretha and Prince Guillaume. Standing are Prince Henri and Prince Jean.

south, deposits of iron ore have created a great steel industry, the country's main source of income.

Agriculture is also of importance, for Luxembourg is a country of small farms. There are various manufacturing plants in the smaller towns as well. Unemployment is not a serious problem in Luxembourg.

The people of Luxembourg love their country, which is rich in historic lore. Castles abound in this land, many of which now lie in ruins. The religious faith of almost all the people is Roman Catholic. The villages and towns are old and quaint, with narrow cobbled streets and old buildings with steep slate-covered roofs.

As we leave lovely, romantic Luxembourg, one thing seems certain: seldom have we had a more interesting journey to any country. Never will we forget our visit to this old, old "Land of Haunted Castles."

ADDENDA

Towns of 1000 Population and Over

There are 30 villages, towns and cities of 1000 or more population in Luxembourg. The largest of them all is the capital city. In order of size, they are:

Luxembourg—80,000
Esch-sur-Alzette—30,000
Differdange—16,500
Dudelange—14,000
Petange—5,500
Schifflange—5,500
Ettelbruck—4,500
Rumelange—4,200
Wiltz—4,100
Diekirch—4,000
Rodange—4,000
Bettembourg—3,500
Echternach—3,300
Kayl—3,100
Grevenmacher—2,800
Walferdange—2,100
Remich—1,800
Wasserbillig—1,800
Mersch—1,500
Lintgen—1,300
Steinfort—1,260
Vianden—1,250
Troisvierges—1,200
Larochette—1,140
Bissen—1,100
Kopstal—1,100
Mondorf-les-Bains—1,100
Wormelange—1,100
Eischen—1,100
Clervaux—1,000

THE LUXEMBOURG NATIONAL ANTHEM

I

Where you see the slow Alzette flow,
the Sura play wild pranks,
where lovely vineyards amply grow
on the Moselle's banks,
there lies the land for which our thanks
are owed to God above,
our own, our native land which ranks
well foremost in our love.

II

In its dark forest's close embrace,
and that of opulent peace
there dwells our hardy, sturdy race
in humble, simple ease.
Though our folks think they have a lease
from liberty to roam
where they are pleased, they never cease
their thoughts of home, sweet home.

III

Our Father in Heaven Whose powerful hand
makes states or lays them low,
protect Thy Luxembourger Land
from foreign foe or woe.
God's golden liberty bestow
On us now as of yore.
Let Freedom's sun in glory glow
for now and evermore.

(Words by Michel Lents. Translated by Nicolas E. Weydert.)

INDEX